MIND

Key Concepts in Philosophy

Key Concepts in Philosophy
Series Editors: John Mullarkey (University of Dundee)
and Caroline Williams (Queen Mary, University of London)

Ethics: Key Concepts in Philosophy, Dwight Furrow
Epistemology: Key Concepts in Philosophy, Christopher Norris
Logic: Key Concepts in Philosophy, Laurence Goldstein,
Andrew Brennan, Max Deutsch, Joe Y. F. Lau
Language: Key Concepts in Philosophy, José Medina

Mind

Key Concepts in Philosophy

Eric Matthews

LONDON • NEW YORK

CONTINUUM

The Tower Building   15 East 26th Street
11 York Road   New York
London SE1 7NX   NY 10010

British Library Cataloguing-in-Publication Data
A catalogue record for this book is available from the British Library.

ISBN 0–8264–7111–0 (hardback)
0–8264–7112–9 (paperback)

Library of Congress Cataloging-in-Publication Data
Matthews, Eric, 1936–
    Mind/by Eric Matthews.
        p. cm. — (Key concept in philosophy)
    Includes bibliographical references and index.
    ISBN 0–8264–7111–0 — ISBN 0–8264–7112–9 (pbk.)
    1. Philosophy of mind.   I. Title.   II. Series.
BD418.3.M355   2005
128′.2 — dc22

2005041399

Typeset by RefineCatch Limited, Bungay, Suffolk
Printed and bound in Great Britain by
MPG Books Ltd, Bodmin, Cornwall

1004730224

CONTENTS

PREFACE

This book is intended to be an introduction to some (but far from all) of the main philosophical topics connected with mind, written for those with little or no previous acquaintance with formal philosophy. Professional philosophers are not the only people who are interested in these topics: they arise in psychology, cognitive science, artificial intelligence, psychiatry and neuroscience, but also in literature, history and indeed ordinary intelligent conversation. The book has been written therefore in a way which I hope will make it readable and interesting to a wider audience than students of philosophy.

As an introduction, it must at least try to survey some of the main currents of thought on this topic. Reasons of space mean that I have not been able to cover by any means all of the possible points of view, but I hope I have covered enough of them to put readers in a position to explore further for themselves. I have given references to authors and works cited in the text in order to make this exploration easier: full bibliographical details of the works cited are given at the end of the book. As far as possible, I have tried to refer to texts which are more readily accessible, at least in libraries: this means, for instance, that I have preferred to cite the reprinted versions of journal papers in widely available anthologies rather than the original version in a journal which might not be easy for many readers to obtain.

In discussing the various points of view, I have tried to present them critically but fairly: philosophy works by argument, and arguments both for and against are presented in as objective a way as I am capable of. But it would be extremely bland and uninteresting if I did not also present the view which I myself favour, and I have done that, starting in Chapter 3. I hope that the arguments for the alternative views are sufficiently well presented to enable readers to make their own judgements about which they find more convincing. The view I favour is not original, in the sense that I am far from the first philosopher to hold it: I have arrived at it partly by simply participating in philosophical discussions with colleagues and students, but partly also under the influence of other philosophers, including those from whom I have learned just because I have disagreed with them so strongly. Some of these influences are apparent in the citations in the text – among these I would mention particularly Merleau-Ponty, Wittgenstein, Ryle and Searle. Others who are not cited, or are only briefly mentioned, would certainly include Hilary Putnam, Charles Taylor, Paul Ricoeur, Hubert Dreyfus, Mary Midgley and the late Stuart Hampshire.

Finally, my thanks are due to my wife Hellen, both for her patience with me while I have been writing this book and for the many conversations we have had about relevant questions. I must also warmly thank my friends Bill Fulford and Martin Wylie for all the good and intellectually stimulating times we have had together.

Eric Matthews
Perthshire
January 2005

CHAPTER 1

MIND AND SOUL

I

What does it mean to be human? Clearly, at its most basic, it means to be a member of a certain biological species, *Homo sapiens*. But the very need which we feel to ask the question suggests that the answer cannot be given in *purely* biological terms: after all, lions don't seem to feel any need to ask what it means to be a lion. Even the standard definition of our species, just referred to, uses the non-biological term *sapiens* (the Latin for 'wise' or 'clever'). Another traditional definition of human beings is that they are 'rational animals', which again neatly combines the biological term 'animal' with the non-biological 'rational'. We *are* certainly animals, primates, like apes and monkeys. But we tend to distinguish ourselves from other primates by our capacity to think things through, to reflect on our own existence and to change our actions in the light of that reflection, to plan and organize our lives, to control our emotions and desires – in short, to be 'rational'. Having these capacities is a large part of what we mean by saying that human beings have 'minds', so we could say that what is distinctive about being human has been held to be that we have minds. It is not surprising, therefore, that central to the Western philosophical tradition has been the attempt to get clearer about what exactly we mean by 'having a mind'. That is what we shall be trying to do in this book: by looking critically at at least some of the central philosophical accounts, we shall seek to give some kind of an answer to the questions: what is it to have a mind? And how is that connected with being human?

To do so requires us to ask a whole set of interlocking questions. Are all 'mental' capacities essentially the same? If so, what is this common essence? Where do we draw the boundaries of the 'mental'? Does 'mind' include non-intellectual characteristics, like emotion or desire? Are mental characteristics all-or-nothing, or can one have them to a greater or lesser degree? Are they unique to human beings, or can other animals have them too, perhaps to a lesser degree? What is the relation between the biological (or physical) and the mental? Are minds 'things', perhaps of a very special kind, which can exist independently of anything biological? Or are they to be identified with parts of our biological organism (nowadays, we would most likely say, with our brains)? Can non-biological beings, like computers or robots, have 'minds'? We shall examine the answers to some of these and related questions given by some leading figures in Western philosophy. But this examination will not be a simple history of ideas: it will involve a critical assessment of the arguments put forward by the figures in question, with a view to forming our own ideas about the nature of mind.

Answering these questions, as said above, is an important part of our attempt to understand ourselves as human beings. That means that they are not mere intellectual puzzles or brain-teasers: they arouse passions because they have a bearing on such things as our attitudes to religion and morality, our view of the relations between ourselves and other animals, or between ourselves and machines, about our individuality and distinctness from each other and the possible relationships we can have with other human beings. The context in which discussions of the nature of mind have taken place has varied from time to time, in tune with the contemporary pre-occupations of human beings with one or other of these issues. Sometimes, philosophers thinking about mind have been more concerned with questions of religion (like 'does the soul survive death?'), at other times with morality ('what is the good for man, and what part is played in it by the human possession of reason?'). At other times, they have been preoccupied rather with distinguishing between human beings and other animals, or alternatively with denying such distinctions. Nowadays, it is very often the question of the difference or similarity between human beings and machines (artificial intelligence), or of the relation between neuroscience and human consciousness, which predominates. The context to some extent changes the terms of the debate, and even the precise meaning of the word 'mind' itself: in order to understand what is said about mind, we may need to see the connection with wider issues. But, as I hope will become clear in the course of the book, there is a common thread running through the whole tradition, from Plato to the present, which links together these different debates into a continuing discussion.

II

A useful starting-point for this discussion would be to reflect on the ways in which we normally talk about our minds, before we begin to do philosophy (or psychology, or neuroscience). Some things in our experience lead us to think of the mental and the physical as totally separate from each other. This way of thinking is reflected in common attitudes and ways of talking. For instance, we talk of a 'triumph of mind over matter', when by a great effort we succeed in overcoming the limitations imposed by our physical nature or by our biologically rooted inclinations. Similarly, we increasingly think it wrong to reduce human beings to their physical characteristics, whether it be the colour of their skin, or their stature, or their gender, their age or whatever. The real person, it seems, is not confined by any such physical limitations, but is expressed in their thoughts, their feelings, their ideals and so on. Sometimes, we even feel detached from our own bodies. Some of these ways of thinking are fairly modern, especially the resistance to stereotyping people in terms of their bodily characteristics, but in other ways this sense of a mind–body distinction has always been present in Western culture, and indeed in many other cultures too.

In the past, though not so much in recent times, this sense of distinction was often expressed in terms of the difference between the 'soul', rather than the 'mind', and the body. In Ancient Greek, the word usually translated into English as 'soul' was *psyche*, from which we derive words like 'psychology' and 'psychiatry'; in Latin, it was *anima*, the source of our words 'animism', 'animated' and the like. We are most familiar with talk about 'souls' in religious contexts, as in the doctrine of the immortality of the soul: the word had that sense in Ancient Greek thought, too, but it also had wider connotations which were not particularly religious.

Psyche or 'soul' for the Greeks meant something that included 'mind', but extended beyond that. Aristotle wrote a treatise *On the Soul* (usually known by its Latin title *De Anima*), in which he equates having a soul simply with being alive, so that even plants and

3

non-human animals have souls. He defines the soul, in this wider sense, by 'the nutritive, perceptive and intellective faculties and movement' (Aristotle 1986: 413b). Of these three kinds of faculties, it is the last, the 'intellective', that we should most naturally identify with 'mind', since it is the capacity to think and reason, to reflect and engage in abstract contemplation, to control one's passions by rational principles, and so on. For Aristotle, only human beings had souls which involved these rational capacities, though their souls shared with those of plants and animals the capacity for self-nutrition, and with animals the capacity for movement and perception. Thus, Aristotle equated 'mind' with a part of the human soul, the most important part, since it was what defined our humanity, but nevertheless not entirely separated from our capacities for biological life and movement.

So what was the 'soul' for Aristotle, and how did it relate to the body? To explain that, we need to say a little about Aristotle's general view of reality. According to him, any individual thing which exists, (a 'substance', in his terminology) requires a 'form' and a 'matter' to make it what it is. That is, it has to be made out of something, its 'matter', and this matter has to be organized in a particular way appropriate to its being the relevant kind of thing, which he called its 'form'. To take one of Aristotle's own examples, an axe is a substance, whose matter is the wood and metal out of which it is made, and whose form is the way in which those materials are combined and shaped to make it capable of fulfilling the function of being an axe. Without both form and matter, it would not exist *as an axe*. A piece of wood and a piece of metal do not constitute an axe until they are combined in the appropriate form; but obviously without material to actualize it, that form would not in itself constitute an axe (at most, it would be the idea of an axe).

In these terms, we can say that a soul, in the broad sense, is the form of a living body. As Aristotle puts it, 'soul is substance as the form of a natural body, which potentially has life' (Aristotle 1986: 412a). In particular, what makes each of us a human being is that we have a soul involving not only nutritive and perceptive powers, but also intellectual or rational faculties: that is, we are living creatures of a certain kind, capable of nourishing ourselves, of moving under our own steam, of responding to the world around us, and above all of thinking and reasoning about our experience. The human soul, on this view, is distinct from the body, in the way that an impression on wax is distinct from the wax (cf. Aristotle 1986: 412b). But it is not a distinct thing or substance from the body: rather, the substance is the human being whose 'matter' is the body and whose 'form' is the soul. In that sense, as Aristotle says, the soul is inseparable from the body: 'soul and body *are* the animal' (Aristotle 1986: 413a).

Aristotle's view of the human soul cannot be fully understood unless we see it as part of what is known as a *teleological*, or purposive, account of reality as a whole. According to this account, briefly, reality is made up of a number of distinct species, or kinds, of things, each with its own place in the scheme of things, its own purpose for existing expressed in the form which defines it as the species it is. The good for each species is to live in accordance with this purpose (so, for example, a good lion is one which best embodies the form of lionhood). The scheme of things is hierarchical, with the human species at the top of the pile. Humanity is defined, as we have seen, by rationality: so the good for humanity is to live a life guided by reason. In this way, Aristotle's account of the human soul was part of a theory of human ethics.

The Aristotelian view was taken up by many medieval thinkers, notably St Thomas Aquinas, and expounded with a number of specifically Christian overtones. But it was generally rejected at the beginnings of modern philosophy in the seventeenth century, by such thinkers as Descartes, Locke, Leibniz and Spinoza, essentially because the teleological background just described did not seem to them to fit with the needs of the modern physical science whose foundations they were trying to elaborate. Nevertheless, there are some things in common between Aristotle's account of the soul and the thinking of some much more recent philosophers about the mind–body problem which we shall be considering in Chapter 3.

We can consider in more detail some of the virtues and vices of this approach in the later chapter, but we need to say something briefly about them here if we are to think critically about Aristotelianism. One of the virtues of the Aristotelian view and its later successors is that it preserves the unity of the human person. Although we do, as was said earlier, have experiences which suggest that we can separate ourselves (our minds) from our bodies – for example, we may be so lost in thought that we do not hear the doorbell ringing – nevertheless, we do not, in non-pathological cases, feel our own bodies to be alien entities, only loosely attached to ourselves, but, as the words themselves imply, *our own* bodies. The fingers with which I am typing these words are *my* fingers, *I* am the one who feels the pressure of the keys on them as I hit each letter. Aristotle's view seems to fit in with this sense of ownership of our own bodies very neatly. My activity of writing this book is an activity neither of my 'mind', nor my 'body', on its own: I could not write it unless I both had thoughts to communicate and some physical way to express those thoughts, in this case, fingers capable of operating a word-processor.

Aristotle's account coheres with this basic intuition of the unity of the person, and that is a very great virtue in it. But it still leaves unanswered a number of important questions about mind–body relations. First, it is all very well to say that a rational soul is the 'form' of a living human body, but that does not in itself tell us what exactly a soul *is*. Literally, 'form' means 'shape', but that is clearly not what Aristotle means by the word in this technical sense. A rational soul is what defines us as human, in combination with a body of a certain kind (a humanoid kind): thus it is not the same as the characteristically human bodily appearance of members of our species. He seems to think of it rather in terms of certain character-istically human *activities* – those same 'mental' activities of thinking, planning, controlling, etc., which were listed at the beginning of the chapter. But, if so, that raises, at least to a modern mind, a further question: are those mental activities to be identified with the oper-ations of certain specific bodily mechanisms (such as brain-processes), or could they be, at least in principle, detached from any such material basis? If the former, then the soul could still be called the 'form' of the human being, and the body the 'matter', but the view would be indistinguishable, apart from its background in Aristotle's teleological view of reality, from any more straight-forwardly 'materialist' account, according to which thoughts, etc., are to be identified simply with brain-processes. On the other hand, if the mental activities are not to be identified with specific bodily mechanisms, then the very basis of Aristotle's account seems to be undermined: he says, after all, that the soul and body cannot exist separately, any more than any other 'form' and 'matter' which together constitute an individual thing as what it is.

Aristotle himself seems more than a little uncertain about this point. After saying that the soul is inseparable from the body, he goes on,

Not that there are not some parts [of the soul] that nothing prevents from being separable, through their not being the actualities of any body. But it remains unclear whether the soul is the actuality of a body in this way or rather is as the sailor of a boat.

(Aristotle 1986: 413a)

The parts of the soul he seems to have in mind are the rational parts, and the uncertainty he seems to be expressing is whether these parts might be separable because they do not depend on (are not actualized in) any particular part of the body – something which he says is still unclear to him. If the rational soul were separable in this way, the unity of soul and body to constitute a person would be destroyed: as he says, the soul would be in the body 'as the sailor of a boat' (this is an image which is very similar to one used by Descartes to convey much the same idea, and we shall come back to it later in the chapter).

III

In the sixteenth and seventeenth centuries AD, the foundations of what we now know as modern science were being laid – not only in the form of particular factual discoveries and the detailed theories to explain them, but also in that of an overall framework of ideas (a 'scientific worldview') into which these facts and theories could be fitted. One of the major preoccupations of early modern philosophers was to provide the basis in philosophical argument for that worldview. It seemed clear to them that the Aristotelian teleological picture of reality, described above, as elaborated by the medieval 'scholastic' philosophers, was quite unsuitable for that purpose. For it depicted a world divided into qualitatively distinct kinds of thing, each with its own 'form', which was supposed to explain its detailed functioning. Why did the flames of a fire rise, while stones fell? Because that was the 'form' or 'nature' of each – that was just how they were, as expressed in their definition. But, the early modern philosophers argued, unless you can specify more precisely what exactly these 'forms' are, then this so-called 'explanation' tells us exactly nothing: it just says, flames rise because that's what they do. In one of his comedies, the contemporary French playwright Molière satirizes this 'scholastic' way of talking by making one of his characters, a doctor, 'explain' the power of opium to put people to sleep by saying it has a 'dormitive power', which is just a fancy way of saying a power to put to sleep. Opium is able to put people to sleep because it is able to put people to sleep: but this is confusing explanation with definition, and a modern scientific view needs to distinguish the two. For a genuine explanation, these philosophers argued, we need some specification of an actual mechanism which would bring about the phenomenon to be explained.

By far the greatest of these early modern philosophers was René Descartes, who both provided the most systematic foundation for a modern scientific worldview and (more relevant to our purposes) elaborated a view of mind in accordance with it which has, in one way or another, dominated much of the thinking about mind since his time. Descartes's account of the mind and its relation to the body is an integral part of his general view of the world, so we shall need to say a little about that first. He aimed, as said earlier, to provide a framework for thinking about the world which would be more 'scientific' (as we should put it) than what had gone before. The great defect, as he saw it, in medieval thought was that it provided no grounds for certainty about anything, because there was no way to decide for sure which (if any) of many competing opinions was true. People appealed to authorities – but that begged the question, *which* authority should we rely on? Or else they accepted uncritically what their senses appeared to tell them: but the senses are notoriously unreliable. If we wanted the kind of reliable knowledge which is essential for anything that could be called a science, Descartes thought, then something drastic needed to be done.

What he proposed was that we should doubt, or call in question, all our beliefs about the world and ourselves, even those that seemed most unquestionable: if, at the end of this process, we could find even one belief that resisted even this intense doubting, then maybe we could take that as a foundation of some sort on which a reliable structure of knowledge could be built. As most people who have read even a little philosophy know, the one and only proposition which Descartes found to resist even the most determined doubt was 'I think, therefore I am', since even to doubt one must exist as a thinking being. He could, if he tried hard enough, doubt the existence of the whole world outside himself; he could even doubt the existence of his own body. The one thing which, by its very nature, it was impossible for him to doubt was his own existence as a thinking thing. This he took to imply that thinking was essential to his existence in a way that, for example, having arms and legs and other bodily attributes (including a brain) was not: he was *essentially* a thing that thinks, a mind.

Thinking does not take up any space, it is 'unextended': it would be absurd to ask, for instance, how many centimetres long my present thought is. So a thinking thing, or mind, can exist without occupying any space at all. On the other hand, a material thing, like a human body, is by definition extended, an occupant of space. (Notice that this means that the Cartesian mind is *not* to be equated with the brain, which is an extended part of the body like any other.) It can't exist without being somewhere in space and occupying a certain volume of space – having length and breadth. Furthermore, a body clearly can exist without thought: a corpse, for example, is still a body, but has no consciousness or thought. So the conclusion seemed to follow that bodies and minds do not need each other to exist – they can exist independently. Descartes says,

> Accordingly this 'I' – that is, the soul by which I am what I am – is entirely distinct from the body, and indeed is easier to know than the body, and would not fail to be whatever it is, even if the body did not exist.
>
> (Descartes 1985: 127)

Descartes's word for something which does not depend on anything else for its existence was a term we have encountered already in discussing Aristotle: 'substance'. So his view was that mind and body are two distinct substances, each of which is therefore capable of existing on its own, without the other. This is the doctrine which is usually called 'Cartesian dualism' ('Cartesian' being the adjectival form of Descartes's name). It is a *dualist* view because it holds, not merely that the mental is different in kind from the physical, but that our mental life takes place in a totally different *thing* from our bodily life: in other words, we have a dual existence. Our mental life, which is our essential self, therefore does not depend on any physical processes, and could possibly go on even if we were no longer alive in a bodily sense. (This clearly fits in well with the religious belief in personal immortality, which it at least makes logically possible.) A living human being, on this view, is made up of two distinct parts, a 'mind' and a 'body'.

Before we go on to consider Cartesian dualism in more detail, it would be useful to contrast it in some key respects with Aristotle's view. Both Descartes and Aristotle agree that soul/mind and body are not identical: but their views about the *way* in which they are distinct are very different. For Aristotle, the *substance*, the independently existing thing, was the human being as a whole, of which soul was the 'form' and body the 'matter'. Neither form nor matter could exist separately from each other, since each could only function in connection with the other. For Descartes, however, as we have just seen, 'mind' and 'body' are *both* substances, and the human being as a whole is simply a composite of two things. Secondly, Descartes, unlike Aristotle, effectively *identifies* 'soul' and 'mind'. Aristotle, as we saw, meant by 'soul' simply the principle of life, including nutritive and perceptive functions as well as those of high-level rational thought. Descartes, by contrast, thinks of the soul entirely in terms of abstract reasoning. In part, this is a result of the way in which he arrived at his conception of mental substance, by separating it from any possibility of contamination with anything physical or bodily. One way in which this difference is clear is that, for Aristotle, *all* living beings have souls of some kind, even plants, whereas for Descartes only *human* beings have them, since only human beings have what Aristotle would have called the intellectual part of the soul. The consequences of this for Descartes's view of the world, and for the modern view of the world generally, are profound and will be explored a little later on.

Mind and body, for Descartes, are not only distinct substances, but totally different *kinds* of thing. Mind is defined entirely in terms of thought, in the most narrow sense: the capacity to be aware of one's own existence, and to have ideas about the existence of other things; the capacity to connect ideas into beliefs, which can be true or false, and to connect beliefs in chains of reasoning; the capacity to remember past ideas; the capacity to form an intention to do something; the awareness of something as desirable or undesirable, agreeable or disagreeable, the kind of thing that might elicit anger, or fear, or love, or hope, or whatever. All of these thoughts are the kind of thing one can have without a body: we can be in a purely intellectual way aware of something, for example, as deserving anger (perhaps because it is an injustice done to us), without necessarily *feeling* anger. But the full-blown emotion of anger clearly does involve feeling as well as thought, and having the feeling involves bodily processes – we feel our cheeks flushing, and our heart pounding, and so on. So, on the Cartesian view, emotions as such (as opposed to their *thought-content*) do not belong to mind, but belong to the inter-action between mind and body (see below). Much the same could be said about desires and wishes: I can have the simple thought that, for example, that apple over there looks good to eat, but having that thought, though it may be necessary, is not sufficient for having a *desire* to eat the apple. To have a full-blown desire for the apple, I must also have a sense of physical need for it, a need to satisfy my body's requirement for food. So again, the Cartesian mind does not include desires in the full sense, but only the thought of certain things as desirable. The Cartesian mind, in short, is to be conceived of as pure intellect or reason.

What about the Cartesian body? Remember it was defined purely in terms of extension, or the occupancy of space; bodies are essentially different from minds, and so their existence does not involve anything mental, anything to do with thought or consciousness. Thus, to explain what goes on in our bodies we need only spatial concepts, and we do not need any concepts involving thought (like the concept of 'purpose', for example). Our bodies, in this sense, are for Descartes just a kind of *machine*, like a clockwork toy, though of course much more complex and sophisticated than such a toy. Suppose we had a clockwork toy drummer: when you wound it up, its hands would move rapidly up and down beating the drum which it held. If this were a *real*, human, drummer, the most natural way to explain his behaviour would be to find the purpose of it – he wants to play in a band, or he wants to attract people to a fairground show. But we don't need to do this in the case of the toy. The toy doesn't have any purposes of its own, it behaves like this simply because that is how its mechanism works. The spring uncoils, causing little cogs to engage with each other inside, so that one cog moves another a certain distance, and eventually this results in the movements of its metal 'arms' which just happen to hit the 'drum', causing drum-like sounds. (Such automata, or mechanical toys, were very fashionable in Descartes's time, and seem to have given him the inspiration for his conception of the body as just a machine: see Descartes 1985: 139 ff.)

So a mind without a body would be pure intellect, while a body without a mind would be just a mechanical system. Many aspects of the behaviour of a living human being, of course, require both mental and bodily processes, both thought and mechanism in collaboration. For example, if am to go for a walk, I must have the intention to do so (thought) and I must actually be able to move my limbs appropriately, which is brought about by processes in my nervous system and muscles (physiological mechanism). But there are some processes which go on in living human beings, in some ways the most basic for biological life, which do not require conscious thought at all, and so which are, in the Cartesian view, purely mechanical. Descartes was thrilled by the recent discovery, by the English scientist William Harvey, of the circulation of the blood, and offers a purely mechanical explanation of how that circulation comes about, in terms of the way the contraction and expansion of the heart, the arteries, veins, membranes, etc., under the influence of heat, force the blood to flow round the body like any other liquid in a hydraulic pumping system (see Descartes 1985: 134 ff.). In the case of non-human animals, their behaviour shows, in Descartes's opinion, that they lack reason and so cannot have a soul. Therefore, he concludes that they are just bodies, i.e. just machines, whose behaviour is no different, except perhaps in degree of complexity, from the kind of automaton we were discussing above.

Part of the motivation for Descartes's dualistic view lies here. He was very interested in improving medicine, in making it, as we would say, more scientific. An important step towards achieving that was to convince people that the human body, except where it interacted with mind, was just a mechanical system. Like any machine, it could go wrong, cease to function properly, or, as we normally say in the case of the body, get sick. Then the rational thing to do, in Descartes's eyes, was the same as with any other machine – identify the fault in the mechanism and try to put it right. Previously, doctors might have thought that the thing to do was to understand the meaning of the illness, the way in which the body was deviating from its natural purpose, and then find some way of restoring it to its proper path. But the Cartesian view was that bodies did not *have* a natural purpose, since only minds can have purposes: they were just machines which could go wrong and needed mechanical intervention. Most modern Western medicine in fact follows this basically Cartesian line, though of course we have a more sophisticated understanding nowadays of things like neurophysiology, biochemistry and so on. But science still tends to think of human and other bodies as mechanisms – it is just that they are vastly more complex mechanisms than the automata that Descartes knew.

Descartes's dualism achieved this by separating mind from body. But this achievement came at a price: the mind must be something purely *non*-mechanical, and have no connection with anything physiological or otherwise physical. It must be an absolutely unique kind of thing, not part of the ordinary universe at all: for everything else in reality is made of the same substance, matter, configured in different ways, but minds alone are not made of matter. Things made of matter, including the human body, are in space, so observable by anyone in the right position, and affect other things in space in accordance with ordinary physical laws (for example, if I kick a football with my foot, the impact causes the football to move in just the same way as the impact of any other similar physical object would). But my mind is supposed by Descartes not to be made of matter, not to be in space, not to be observable therefore by anyone except myself, and not to be able to cause movement in physical objects in accordance with ordinary physical laws.

So we have here a whole picture of the world, of which the picture of human minds, human bodies and their relationship forms only a part (though a very important part). On the one hand, we have minds, which think about the world and the objects in it (we might call this the 'subjective' side of the picture). On the other, we have the world and the objects that minds think about (this is the 'objective' side). The objective world has a unity to it: it is all made of the same stuff ('matter'), and so everything that takes place in it is governed by the same set of ultimate laws, the laws of physics. Our human bodies are part of this objective world, and are governed by the same physical laws as any other part; but our essential selves, or minds, are like disconnected points outside the objective world and its laws, from which that world can be viewed. To use a modern image, our minds are no more part of the world we observe than people in a cinema audience are part of the 'world' of the film they are watching. What goes on on the 'screen' before us is independent of any thoughts or feelings we may have about it from our seat in the back row. This view of the world does indeed fit in very well with the requirements of a modern scientific approach, both in its suggestion of a single, law-governed physical world (unlike the qualitatively diverse world of Aristotle), and in its implication that what goes on objectively in the world is independent of how we may subjectively think or feel about it.

IV

This consistency with the kind of picture of the world which was required by the new sciences which were developing at the time – a development in which Descartes himself played a prominent part – was one of the attractions of Cartesian mind–body dualism. Connected with this was the way, mentioned above, in which it seemed to provide a better framework for an effective medicine than previous views of the body and its relation to the mind. Some have also seen one of the attractions of this form of dualism in the way it seems to provide philosophical support for some of the basic doctrines of the Christian religion, such as the immortality of the soul and the freedom of the will. Descartes himself mentions the demonstration of the possibility of immortality as one of the benefits of his position in the 'Dedicatory Letter' at the beginning of his *Meditations on First Philosophy* (see Descartes 1984: 3–6). It is obvious that, if the soul is a distinct 'substance' from the body and so capable of existing independently of it, it does not *necessarily* cease to exist when the body dies (whether it *actually* continues existing could then be a matter for faith, rather than philosophy). As for freedom of the will, if the soul is not part of the physical world and so not governed by the laws of physical science, then what we choose to do is not governed by, or predictable in terms of, those physical laws, and in that sense is free.

But a philosophical doctrine cannot be defended simply because it is attractive as a support for religion, or even for science and medicine: it has to have valid *arguments* in its favour, and to stand up to reasonable *objections* to it. Descartes's main argument in favour of his dualism starts with his 'method of doubt' – the method of subjecting all our seemingly most obvious beliefs to question – and its conclusion in the one indubitable proposition 'I think, therefore I am' and the implications which he draws from it. We can doubt any other belief at all, he argues first, even our belief that there is a world and that we have a body, but even to do so implies that our existence as a purely thinking thing is not open to question. Having to his own satisfaction established that, he goes on with the next stage. Since, he argues, we can conceive of the non-existence of our bodies but cannot conceive of our own non-existence as thinking things or minds, the existence of ourselves as minds must be independent of that of our bodies or anything else which is material, that is, mind and matter are distinct substances.

How good is this argument? Let us take the two stages separately. First, is it really the case – *could* it be the case – that the only proposition we could not possibly doubt is the one which affirms our own existence as purely thinking beings? Many philosophers have pointed out that doubting one thing presupposes that one does not doubt others. For really to doubt something requires some reason for doubting it, and that reason must be something one does not doubt. For example, suppose someone is in the middle of the desert and dying of thirst: they think that they can see an oasis in the distance, with pools of water and palm trees. Quite reasonably, they might doubt whether this was a *real* oasis or just a mirage, a trick of the light given form by their own intense longing for water. But this doubt only makes sense because they do not doubt other things – that they are in the desert, that mirages of this kind do occur in such conditions, and so on. These are their *reasons* for doubting, and doubt without reasons isn't really doubt in any meaningful sense. To doubt the whole existence of everything outside oneself all at once, therefore, seems to be impossible, because it removes all sense from the idea of doubting.

Doubting, in short, takes place against the background of a world which is not doubted. In particular, to have doubts about the existence of anything outside oneself seems to presuppose that one does not doubt that one is *in* the world, that is, that one has a physical position in it, given by one's own body. Thus, the possibility of doubting the existence of one's own body seems particularly meaningless. (It is true that people suffering from certain pathological mental conditions do genuinely doubt the existence of their own bodies: but it is significant that this is *pathological* doubt, not the kind of doubt as a method of reaching philosophical certainty which Descartes claims to practise.)

A similar objection to Descartes's argument is this: it is questionable whether it could be the case that the *only* thing I was certain of was my own existence as a thinking being, and that everything outside my own thoughts was open to doubt. To think, after all, one must think *about something* – one's thoughts have some reference beyond themselves (otherwise, what distinguishes one thought from another?). Descartes himself accepts this: my certainty of my own existence as a thinking being includes my certainty that I have the *thoughts* of things outside myself. It may be open to doubt whether the word-processor I seem to be typing these words on actually exists, but it is not open to doubt, he would say, that *it seems to me as if it exists*, that I have the 'idea' of such a word-processor in my mind. But this raises the question of where these ideas come from. Descartes sometimes talks as if at least our most general ideas about the world are 'innate', that is, are as it were built into the very fabric of our minds themselves. But even if one accepted that about our most general ideas – ideas of extension and consciousness, of things and their qualities, etc. – it would still need to be explained why at this moment I have ideas of this specific word-processor, of the desk in my study, of the sunlight streaming through the trees outside my window and so on. Normally, we would say that I have such ideas at this moment because of the way in which my bodily senses are responding to current stimulation. Sometimes, it is true, I may have such ideas without appropriate current stimulation, as when I hallucinate or when I dream: but, following the argument set out just above, it can make sense to talk about hallucinations or illusions only against a general background in which one is *not* hallucinating or dreaming. If this is right, then one could not even have the certainty of one's own existence as a thinking being unless one also had the certainty that one existed in the world as a physical being with bodily senses.

Finally, one could use a certain interpretation of Wittgenstein's argument against the possibility of a purely private language against Descartes on this point (see Wittgenstein 1953: I 243 ff). Descartes pictures himself, at the end of his process of questioning everything, as left with only the certainty of his own thoughts and their contents. But to have that certainty, he must have a language in which to state it (and of course he *does* have such a language, in which he expresses his conclusions in his books). Since he is at this stage doubting whether anything outside his own thoughts, including other people, actually exists, this language must be purely private: that is, the words in it must be given their meaning by Descartes himself, independently of their use to communicate with others. He alone really knows what he means by 'mind', 'thought', 'world', 'God' and so on. But Wittgenstein argued that such a purely private language was impossible. For to say that a particular expression, say, 'book', *means* something is, he argued, to say that there is a rule governing when it can properly be applied and when it can't. For example, 'book' can be applied to my copy of Descartes's works lying beside me, but not to the plant-pot sitting on my desk. If there were no such rules, then no term would have any meaning at all – that is, the sounds we uttered would not constitute a language.

But these rules can't be purely private: I can't have my own set of rules, because then it would be a matter for my own arbitrary decision whether a particular expression was being appropriately applied or not, and a 'rule' which works by arbitrary decision isn't really a rule. A rule requires some kind of objective check of correct application, and that implies that rules must be shared with others, who can, for example, correct me when I call the plant-pot a 'book'. So again, if this objection is sound, then Descartes could not be certain even of his own thoughts unless he was also certain of the existence of other people to whom he could, in principle, communicate these thoughts in a shared language.

The second stage of Descartes's argument for dualism depends on the conclusion of the first, and so is inevitably weakened if that conclusion does not follow. His argument here is that we can doubt whether our bodies exist, but cannot doubt whether we exist as thinking beings, and so that we could exist as purely thinking things without bodies. But clearly, if the objections to the first stage are sound, then the premise of this argument has not been established – it might be that our existence as thinking beings is dependent on our having bodies, so that the second stage cannot even get started. But even if we ignore that problem, does the second stage argument really work as it stands, anyway? Descartes's first critics, and many since his time, have pointed out that, from the fact, if it is a fact, that we can doubt the existence of our bodies but not our own existence as thinking things, it does not follow that it is logically possible for our thinking selves to exist even if our bodies did not.

For instance, in his objections to Descartes's argument in the *Meditations*, one of the very earliest critics, Antoine Arnauld, uses this analogy: suppose someone knows for certain that something is a right-angled triangle, but (as is perfectly possible) doubts, or even denies, Pythagoras's theorem, that the square on the hypotenuse in a right-angled triangle is equal to the sum of the squares on the other two sides. Then he may construct an argument of exactly the same structure as Descartes's argument about mind and matter. The argument, as stated by Arnauld, goes like this:

I clearly and distinctly perceive that the triangle is right-angled; but I doubt that the square on the hypotenuse is equal to the squares on the other two sides; therefore it does not belong to the essence of the triangle that the square on the hypotenuse is equal to the squares on the other sides

(see Descartes 1984: 142).

The analogical argument is clearly invalid, since both the premises might be true but the conclusion is false. So Descartes's argument, which has the same structure, must also be invalid. What we find it possible or impossible to doubt tells us nothing about what actually exists, or what might or might not depend for its existence on something else. The fact that I can *say* that I doubt the existence of my own body, but cannot say I doubt the existence of myself does not prove that I could really exist without a body, but only that I may be ignorant of the real dependence of my thought on bodily processes.

Descartes's positive argument for his form of dualism, therefore, does not seem to prove his point. But to say that does not amount to disproving his view: there might, after all, be other, stronger, arguments in favour of it. More important is to see whether he can withstand some possible objections to his position. The objections which will be considered here will be some of the standard ones: they have something in common, namely, that they all claim that Cartesian dualism cannot account for some things which seem to many people to be obvious about human minds and bodies. The assumption behind this kind of objection is that, if dualism were true, then it ought to be able to give a satisfactory account of such obvious facts. But of course one could reject such objections either because one did not accept this underlying assumption (one could argue that dualism could after all account for the facts in question) or because one didn't regard the allegedly obvious facts as really obvious at all. One might also simply reject the assumption that it is a fault in a philosophical theory if it cannot always fit in what look like obvious facts: but that would be a move which needed further justification of its own.

The allegedly unaccounted for facts which will be considered here are: the fact of mind–body interaction; the unity of the human personality; the existence of unconscious mental processes; the similarities between the mental processes of human beings and other animals, as revealed for instance by evolutionary biology; and the dependence of thought-processes on the workings of the brain, as revealed by an increasingly sophisticated neuroscience. The ... two sorts of fact are different from the others, in that they are part of ordinary experience, and do not depend for their appreciation, like the others, on developments in more specialist scientific areas (though the third kind of fact, about the unconscious, could be said to straddle the divide between ordinary experience and science).

Our mental and our physical lives do seem obviously to interact in various ways. When we have indigestion (a bodily state), we may feel irritable (a mental disposition); when we are in love with someone (a mental state), our hearts may race (a bodily condition). When I very much want that apple on the higher branches of the tree, that mental wanting may cause me to reach out my arm (part of my body) in an attempt to pluck it. Or when someone has suffered a brain injury, that may cause them to lose memory, or even to undergo a radical change of personality. All these things are parts of our common experience, and surely, it might be argued, any satisfactory philosophical account of the nature of mind and its relation to the body ought to be able to fit them in. The first, and probably the most common, objection to Cartesian dualism is that it cannot do this.

If minds and bodies are not only distinct things, but totally different kinds of substances, the objection goes, then there is no way in which it is possible to explain such simple everyday phenomena as that in which I decide to raise my arm and this decision causes my arm to rise. For the movements of my arm belong to the physical world, the world of material substance, where everything can be explained, according to Cartesian dualism, in terms of the laws of a mechanistic physics. But my thoughts, e.g. my decision to raise my arm, belong, according to that same dualism, to the quite different world of mental substance, which is not governed by the laws of mechanistic physics (and perhaps not by any kind of laws at all other than the laws of logic). So how can we explain how something going on in one world can cause something going on in the other?

The examples given in which the mind is experienced as influencing the body are all cases of emotion, desire and will, which, as we saw, are strictly not part of the Cartesian mind. For Descartes, the mind is equated with pure intellect or thought. But this brings out the problem, if anything, even more starkly. Take the case in which I decide to raise my arm. Suppose a teacher asks those who know the answer to a question to put their hands up; I think I know the answer, so I decide to raise my hand. According to Descartes's picture, what must go on is that I have the pure thought of raising my arm and then this somehow causes something of a totally different kind, namely, the appropriate movement of my arm from its hanging position to an upward-pointing position. The question is, what can be meant by 'causes' in this context?

Normally, our attribution of causes is based on a background of generalizations and a sense of the *way* in which the cause leads to the effect. Consider a philosophically standard example of one physical event causing another: a billiard ball striking another and causing it to move a certain distance in a particular direction. We know intuitively (though we could also, if we wanted to, spell it out more precisely in terms of laws of physics) that this is what generally happens when one billiard ball strikes another with this force from this direction: it is this kind of intuitive knowledge which the billiards player draws on in setting up his shots. And we know *how it works* – it is the impact of the one billard ball on the other which makes the other one move: this is part of our intuitive understanding of how the physical world behaves. Neither intuitive nor scientific understanding of physics, however, can come into play in mind–body interactions if Descartes is right, because the mind is not part of the physical world. It is not even true that every time I have the thought of moving some part of my body the appropriate part moves in accordance with my thought. This may fail to happen, for instance because of paralysis. But can we account for this in terms of Descartes's view?

Descartes himself recognizes the problem of interaction, and attempts to offer a solution. There is a body in the middle of the brain called the pineal gland: in Descartes's time, and for long after, it was not clear what the function of this body was, though neuroscientists now have a better understanding of it. Descartes thought that this body might be the point of contact between mind and body, the point at which thought-messages from the mind were realized in movements in the brain and through that in the nerves and muscles. But no such solution could really work: the pineal gland is part of the brain, and so part of the physical world – it occupies space, and so cannot belong to the mental realm as Descartes defines it. So the problem is not solved, only shifted: it now becomes the question of how what goes on in the mind can cause movements of a physical body like the pineal gland.

Attempts have been made by followers of Descartes to show

how our experience of mind–body interaction can be accounted for within a dualist framework. Most of these involve denying that the interaction is genuinely *causal* in the normal sense that was explained just now. For examples, the late seventeenth-century French philosopher, Nicolas Malebranche (1638–1715), proposed the theory called 'occasionalism'. When I decide to raise my arm and my arm rises, Malebranche maintained, it was not so much that my decision *caused* my arm movement, but that God arranged things so that, on the 'occasion' of my decision, my arm moved appropriately. Perhaps a partial analogy might be something like this: you and I might have a system such that, when I flashed a particular light-signal to you, you would then raise a flag. My light-signal would not directly *cause* the raising of the flag, but would be the *occasion* on which you would raise the flag. An obvious objection to occasionalism, as a general theory of mind–body interactions, is that it requires us to invoke quite arbitrarily the constant action of God, simply in order to sustain dualism as an account of the nature of mind: that is surely a purely ad hoc device. Furthermore, occasionalism cannot really explain why sometimes decisions are not followed by appropriate actions, except by appealing to the mysterious purposes of God, and that seems bizarre for such an everyday phenomenon.

A slightly different attempt can be seen in the theory of 'pre-established harmony' put forward by Leibniz (1646–1716). This does not require constant activity by God, just that God might have arranged things from the beginning in such a way that what happened in the mind ran parallel with what happened in the body (it would be possible equally simply to assume that such parallelism just happens as a matter of fact, without involving divine intervention at all). An analogy which Leibniz himself uses is of a clockmaker who winds up two clocks at the same time, so that whenever one clock shows noon, the other one does too. The time on the first clock does not *cause* that on the second clock, but it is always possible to predict the time on one clock from that on the other. So, on this view, it would just happen (perhaps because God willed it to be so) that, when I had the thought, 'I must raise my arm', my arm rose. But again, this seems an incredibly contrived way to account for something as ordinary as deciding and acting on one's decision. And again, it does not really explain why the parallelism does not always work.

Unless some better solution can be found to the problem of mind–body interaction, then, this seems to be a serious weakness in

Cartesian dualism. The interaction of mind and body in the way described is one instance of the experienced unity of human beings. We do not normally feel ourselves to be minds loosely attached to bodies, to be 'lodged in our bodies like a pilot in a ship', as Descartes himself puts it (cf. the similar phrase used by Aristotle and quoted earlier in the chapter). As we said before, this arm is *my* arm, the arm I use to work with, to wave to people, to embrace those I love and so on: if I cut it, *I* am the one who feels the pain. Significantly, Descartes recognizes this feeling and seems to share it (see Descartes 1984: 56). The trouble is that his own dualism seems to imply precisely that 'pilot in a ship' relation to our own bodies. If I am identical with my mind, and if my mind is a mental substance, independent in its existence from body, then it follows that I am independent in my existence from my own body, just as a pilot's existence is independent of the existence of his ship. I am not, as in Aristotle's account, distinct from my body simply as form from matter, where both form and matter are necessary to make an individual person. Rather, my existence as a person is entirely contained in my mind, and my body is simply a loosely attached appendage of myself, in this life anyway, which will be shed, as in many religious systems, when my body dies and I go on existing. How plausible one finds this view depends on whether one prefers our ordinary intuitions of mind–body unity to this kind of spiritualism or vice versa.

The other problems for Cartesian dualism mentioned earlier are all, as was said then, to do with scientific developments in our understanding of human beings. One development in the last hundred years or so has been our greater awareness of the role of *unconscious* mental processes in affecting our behaviour: unconscious thoughts, unconscious desires and motives, unconscious fantasies and so on. It was Freud who did most to make the idea of 'the unconscious' fashionable, though it is arguable (and Freud himself sometimes affirms this) that there has always been a certain recognition that not everything about the mind is fully conscious. For Descartes, however, thought and other mental processes are *by definition* conscious: the soul, as he says in the quotation given earlier, is 'easier to know than the body' (Descartes 1985: 127). Everything that is in the mind is 'clear and distinct', so that unconscious mental processes are logical impossibilities, contradictions in terms. It may of course be that one could find some way of describing the phenomena we call 'unconscious' in some other way which would be consistent with

Descartes's definition of the mental: but, short of that, this seems like a serious difficulty with Cartesian dualism.

Part of the tendency in our thinking about ourselves which has led to the emphasis on the unconscious is probably an increasing recognition of the similarities between at least some of our mental processes and those of other animals, especially our closest relatives, the great apes. Once the Darwinian thesis that we had evolved from other species by natural selection had been generally accepted, it was a natural step to see our mental capacities as having evolved likewise. Darwin himself took that step in his great work *Expression of the Emotions in Man and Animals* (1872). Cartesian dualism, however, as we have seen, makes a sharp distinction between human beings and other animals, who, lacking reason, are mere automata, like the mechanical toys with which Descartes was familiar. If there is such a sharp leap from animals to human beings, then it is hard to see how the transition could be accomplished in an evolutionary way. Darwinism is, of course, an empirical scientific theory, and may not necessarily be true: but, for anyone who regards it as one of the great achievements of modern science, the fact that Cartesian dualism fits in with it so badly seems to call in question, to say the least, the plausibility of dualism.

Finally, the more we know about the workings of our brain, the more convincing it seems that our thought-processes are heavily dependent on those workings: certain kinds of brain damage lead to loss of memory, others to loss of the power of speech; people's personalities change as a result of brain damage; when brains are scanned by the PET (positron emission tomography) scanners used in modern medical diagnosis to give an image of the interior workings of the brain, particular parts of the brain 'light up' when particular sorts of mental activity go on; and so on. Descartes himself clearly saw a relation between brain activity and mental activity. But his conception of the mind sharply distinguishes it from the brain, as from other parts of the body: and this distinction is so sharp, that it is hard to see how he can account for the apparent dependence of mind on brain (and indeed of brain on mind). This is a particular form of the problem of mind–body interaction, and it is this form above all which has led, as we shall see in the next chapter, to a certain kind of reaction against Cartesian dualism, in the name, ironically, of precisely that modern scientific view of the world which Descartes himself did so much to establish.

CHAPTER 2

MINDS AND BRAINS

I

We experience ourselves and other people as having both a mental and a bodily life: as thinking, feeling, wishing, deciding, remembering and so on (the 'mental' life), and also as breathing, eating, digesting, walking, sleeping and so on (the 'bodily' life). Furthermore, it is one and the same person who decides to go for a walk and who then walks. Some of our activities have both a mental and a physical side to them: seeing, for example, requires both the impact of light on our retina and consequent nervous activity and also a consciousness or awareness of seeing and a recognition of what it is we are seeing. But Cartesian dualism, as we have seen, treats the mental and the bodily as distinguishable from each other, belonging to separate 'substances'. This seemed misguided even to some of Descartes's earliest critics. Apart from the problems of accounting for mind–body interaction which have already been mentioned, there seems to be a possible offence against a widely accepted principle of philosophy, usually called 'Occam's Razor' (after the medieval English philosopher, William of Occam). The principle can be stated as: do not multiply entities beyond necessity. In other words, do not postulate more kinds of thing than you really need to in order to account for a phenomenon.

Descartes could be seen as offending against this principle in that he introduces a mysterious extra entity, 'mental substance', in order to account for human behaviour, when perhaps we could account for it all without this extra entity, simply by saying that human beings are material things like any other, and that their behaviour can be adequately explained simply by using the same physical, chemical, etc., laws which we use to explain the behaviour of other material things. Descartes himself had said that human behaviour, in so far as the mind was not involved, was like that of the mechanical automata which were fashionable in his own day: but why, his critics argued, should we not say that human beings were like automata (no doubt, extremely complex automata) in all respects, even those in which thought was involved? Wouldn't that produce a much simpler and more elegant account of nature, in which human behaviour and the behaviour of everything else were all ultimately explained by the same set of laws? The view that the mental life of human beings is a physical process like everything else is what might be called 'classical materialism' or 'classical physicalism'.

The desire for a single unified explanation of everything is a crucial part of what we can recognize as the modern scientific approach to the world, which Descartes himself had helped to found. And as that modern scientific approach became more widespread, so did the materialist critique of Cartesian dualism. This kind of criticism can be seen in Descartes's contemporaries, such as Hobbes, Gassendi and Locke (who asked why God could not have added a capacity for thought to matter, without the need for a separate thinking substance). But it became really widespread in the eighteenth century, in the movement known as the Enlightenment, which aimed to replace what it regarded as old-fashioned superstitions by a view of things based on scientific reason. The title of one of the best-known works by the Enlightenment figure Julien de la Mettrie was *L'Homme machine* (Machine Man) (first published in 1747: for a recent English translation, see La Mettrie 1996): as his title suggests, La Mettrie describes human beings as simply very complex bits of machinery. He held that the only sure way to arrive at whatever kind of truth we could on this or other matters was to use observation, rather than *a priori* reasoning of Descartes's kind. On this basis, he denied that we could have any clear idea of human nature. In particular, all we could say about the soul was something very vague, namely, that it is whatever it is in us which is responsible for thinking. Empirical research, he argued, would show that ordinary principles of movement could account not only for physical motion, but also for such things as thought and perception. The different temperaments of different people could be seen to correspond to physical differences, and mental disorder had long been thought to be caused by changes in the balance of the 'humours' in the body (changes in the body's biochemistry, as we might say), or to problems in brain functioning. The differences between human beings and other animals can be seen to be matters of degree: human beings can do things which other animals cannot, such as geometrical reasoning, only, La Mettrie argues, because they have bigger brains and because they have learned to do these things – a human being becomes an author, to use one of his examples, just as a donkey becomes a beast of burden. The conclusion drawn from all these considerations is that man is a machine, and that there is only one substance, matter, whose different modifications produce the variety of things which we see.

II

To understand these historical origins of modern materialism is important if we are to see the attraction of more recent developments. Materialism continues to be associated with a belief in modern science and its capacity to explain everything about the world and ourselves that we might wish or need to explain. The science to which La Mettrie appealed was crude and in a very early stage of its development. But in the centuries between his time and ours, and especially in the latter half of the twentieth century, our knowledge of the brain and its workings, though still imperfect, has developed to a much higher level of sophistication. Probably in part because of this, there has in recent years been a revival of various forms of materialism in the analytic movement in philosophy. One of the earliest examples of this was the 'mind–brain identity thesis', developed by a number of thinkers in the 1950s. To explain what this thesis was, we cannot do better than examine one of its first expressions in print, an article by U. T. Place with the title 'Is consciousness a brain-process?', which appeared in the *British Journal of Psychology* in 1956 (references here to its reprinted version, Place 2002). Place contends that 'we can identify consciousness with a given pattern of brain activity': this is described, not as a philosophical conclusion from *a priori* reasoning, but as 'a reasonable scientific hypothesis' (Place 2002: 55). There would be scientific grounds for accepting it, Place holds, if the empirical evidence suggested that we could 'explain the subject's introspective observations by reference to the brain-processes with which they are correlated'.

What Place is looking for is an alternative to dualism, a way of avoiding any suggestion that we need to postulate a separate 'mind' in order to account for any aspect of human experience or behaviour. Many aspects of human mental life, he argues, can be dealt with in a clearly non-dualistic fashion by means of the doctrine known as 'logical behaviourism'. More will be said about this doctrine in the next chapter, but for the moment we can summarize it as the doctrine that statements about some apparently mental phenomenon can be translated into statements about our dispositions to behave in certain ways. For example, 'John's overriding aim is to make a lot of money from his business' could be translated as 'If presented with an opportunity to make money from his business, John is likely to seize it': the 'translation' has, a behaviourist would say, the same meaning as the original, but, unlike it, makes no use of such 'mentalistic' terms as 'has the overriding aim', but refers only to what John can actually be seen to do in certain circumstances.

However, Place recognizes that there are some uses of mentalistic concepts which can't be so easily dealt with in this behaviouristic way: such things as consciousness, experience, sensation or mental imagery. These seem, by their very nature, not to be equivalent to any tendency shown in externally observable behaviour, but to be going on at a particular moment and in some way 'inside' the individual concerned. When I feel pain, for instance, I may be so stoical that I do not give vent to my pain in any way which others can observe – I may not even say that I feel pain. I may even act in an outward way which belies the pain I feel inside. Conversely, I can pretend to feel pain when in fact I feel nothing at all. In that sense, my feelings are private to me: no one else can tell, by simple observation of my behaviour, whether or not I am feeling pain (or happiness, or pleasure, or anger or whatever). In much the same way, it is impossible to tell from observing my outward behaviour alone whether I am having mental images, and if so what they are images of; or whether I am having the conscious experience which is appropriate for the way I am behaving. This privacy of our subjective experience might seem, Place admits, to be an argument in favour of dualism, from which it follows that there is a gap between inward mental experience and its outward manifestations in bodily movements. If we are to reject dualism, therefore, we must show how it is possible to give a non-dualist account of such private or inner states.

Place's own account, as said above, is proposed, not as a philosophical doctrine, but as a scientific hypothesis: the suggestion is that future scientific research might well lead us to the conclusion that conscious experience is identical with brain-processes, rather than with states of some non-physical 'mental substance'. Brain-processes are, of course, *literally* inside us and hidden from at any rate ordinary observation. He compares it to the way in which science has led us to identify lightning, not (as in the superstitious past) with the anger of the gods, but with the motion of electrical charges in the atmosphere. Just as in that case, the more scientific identification would tidy up our account of the world, producing a single coherent account of things in which all phenomena could ultimately be explained by relatively few laws. There would not be, to use a phrase of another identity theorist, Herbert Feigl, any 'nomological danglers' ('nomological' comes from the Greek word for 'law', *nomos*): that is, any *special* laws required for explaining particular classes of phenomena (lightning or consciousness) which did not fit together with the laws we used to explain other phenomena (such as electric lights or digestive problems).

If this is a scientific hypothesis, where does philosophy come in? Place gives philosophy a mainly negative role: he aims, in his paper, to show that there are no philosophical arguments which would enable anyone to *dismiss* the hypothesis as logically impossible. For example, one standard philosophical argument against identifying consciousness with brain-processes is that the expression 'consciousness' clearly does not *mean the same* as the expression 'brain-process'. This is shown by the fact that people have been able to talk perfectly well for thousands of years about their states of consciousness ('I feel angry about this', 'I feel a deep sense of inner calm', etc.) without knowing anything about the processes which go on in their brain, indeed without even knowing or believing that the brain has anything to do with consciousness. Both they and their hearers knew perfectly well what they meant, so what they meant can't have had anything to do with the brain.

Place accepts this completely, but denies that it has anything to do with the thesis he is putting forward. The argument just given certainly proves that consciousness is not identical with brain-processes in the way that, say, triangles are the same thing as three-sided plane figures. 'Triangles are three-sided plane figures' is a logically necessary truth, so that the identity here is a *necessary* one: someone who denied it would make a logical mistake, showing that they did not really understand what is meant by the word 'triangle'. For that reason, it can be proved by pure *a priori* reasoning. But 'lightning is a motion of electrical charges' is a statement of identity which is not necessary, but contingent. Someone who denies it is making (as we now think) a factual, not a logical, mistake; and it cannot therefore be proved to be true by pure reasoning, but only by empirical investigation. The same is true, Place wants to argue, of 'consciousness is a brain-process': this too, according to him, is a statement of *contingent*, not of *necessary*, identity. (Something is 'contingently' true when it only *happens* to be true and might conceivably be false). It needs to be proved (or disproved) empirically, because, as Place puts it, 'the operations which have to be performed in order to verify the presence of the two sets of characteristics inhering in the object or state of affairs in question can seldom if ever be performed simultaneously' (Place 2002: 57). We can establish that lightning is a motion of electrical charges only by observing lightning by sight and then detecting by some other means that it occurs only when there is a motion of electrical charges in the atmosphere: this leads us to explain the visual observation by the motion of electricity. In much the same way, Place hypothesizes, we shall observe that people only have conscious experience when certain processes take place in their brains, and this will lead us to see that the brain-processes fully explain the conscious experience, that nothing non-physical needs to be postulated to account for them.

Another objection to the identity thesis considered by Place has been put forward by neurophysiologists like Charles Sherrington, though it is essentially philosophical in character. This is the argument that it seems difficult to account for something like the subjective experience of having, say, a sensation of red in terms of brain-processes, the firing of neurons, which are not themselves red. This objection, Place replies, is based on what he calls 'the phenomenological fallacy', the mistaken idea that describing what appears to us is describing 'something going on in a mysterious internal environment' (Place 2002: 55). That is, Sherrington is assuming that saying 'I have a sensation of red' is saying 'There is something going on inside me which is red'. What we should rather say, according to Place, is that having a sensation of red is responding as one normally would do if one were seeing something red outside oneself. It is not the *sensation* which is identical with a brain-process, but the *having* of the sensation, which is not red or any other colour, and that seems much easier to account for in terms of what goes on in the brain.

III

Another well-known advocate of the identity thesis is the Australian philosopher J. J. C. Smart: Smart's discussion of the thesis is similar to Place's in many ways, but has some differences. In his paper 'Sensations and brain-processes' (Smart 2004), Smart makes it plain from the outset that he is motivated by respect for the scientific view of the world: increasingly, he points out, the findings of the sciences make it possible for us to see living organisms, including human organisms, as nothing more than physico-chemical mechanisms. But Smart, like Place, makes the point that one thing about human beings which might not seem, at least at first sight, to fit this description is *consciousness*, the apparently inner awareness we have which is not obviously expressed in our outward behaviour: Smart's example is having an after-image. When someone, for instance, looks at something yellowish-orange and then closes their eyes, they may still seem to see a yellowish-orange patch: this may be described as 'having a yellowish-orange after-image'. This after-image seems to be something private to the individual concerned, something which they alone can see, and there is nothing about their outward behaviour which could give anyone else a clue that this is what they are experiencing. And if you opened up their head, you would not see anything yellowish-orange in there. All this seems to suggest that an after-image must be something non-physical.

If we accept this, however, then, Smart argues, we are excluding after-images and similar things entirely from the unified scientific theory which seems to cover everything else in the world. Smart uses the phrase we have already quoted from Herbert Feigl: after-images interpreted in this way are 'nomological danglers' – they are loose ends which cannot be fitted in under the normal laws of physical science. But the idea that there should be real things which are outside the scope of a unified science seems to Smart to be, in his own words, 'frankly unbelievable'. This is what motivates him to see whether there are any good reasons for believing it – in other words, for accepting Cartesian dualism. Like Place, Smart is philosophical in an essentially *negative* way: he does not offer philosophical arguments *in favour* of materialism: materialism will, in his view, be accepted by any reasonable, scientifically minded person, as long as it can be shown that there are no good philosophical reasons for accepting that the mental realm is exceptional, in that it cannot be fitted in to a single materialist framework. Smart's aim is 'to show that there are no philosophical arguments which compel us to be dualists' (Smart 2004: 118).

There are it seems for Smart only three possible alternatives to dualism. First, there is behaviourism, which he would regard as inadequate for much the same reasons as Place. Secondly, there is what Smart calls a Wittgensteinian 'expressive' analysis of what look like reports of conscious states: on this analysis, saying 'I have a pain in my stomach' is not reporting something called a 'pain', but is a verbal substitute for the natural non-verbal ways of expressing pain, such as crying out, screwing up one's face, holding the affected part and so on. Smart rejects this expressive analysis because he sees no reason for denying that 'I have a pain' or 'I have an after-image' is just as much of a genuine report as saying, e.g., 'I have a rash on my foot'. This seems to him to leave only one possibility: that conscious experiences, like having pains or other sensations, or having after-images, just *are* brain-processes – that they are literally and strictly identical with what goes on in the brain when one has these experiences. A dualist might accept that conscious experiences are always *correlated with* brain-processes (as in Malebranche's occasionalism or Leibniz's pre-established harmony: see Chapter 1): but something can only be said to be 'correlated with' something else if it is distinct from it. Smart wants to see if there is any good reason for thinking that conscious experiences must be distinct from brain-processes.

He considers several reasons which have traditionally been offered for thinking this (some of these have already been mentioned in connection with Place's article, so we shall consider here only the *new* points that Smart makes about them). First, there is the familiar argument that people can talk about after-images, etc., without knowing anything about the brain. But that, Smart argues, only shows, if it shows anything, that we can know what 'after-image' means without knowing anything about neurophysiology. Equally, he would say, we can talk about lightning without knowing anything about electricity: but that doesn't prove that lightning is something different from electrical discharges in the atmosphere. Science shows us, Smart would say, that that is what lightning *really is*, and no one would nowadays deny the scientific view simply on the grounds that generations of people were able to refer to lightning without knowing anything about science. Why therefore should we draw this conclusion about consciousness and brain-processes?

This leads on to the second objection. Smart is claiming that it might turn out to be the case that as science develops we are led to the conclusion that consciousness is nothing more than brain-processes. But scientific claims, the objector says, are by their very nature *falsifiable*: they are just hypotheses, which might turn out to be false in the light of new evidence. So no matter what the evidence might now seem to point to, it might be that the identity thesis was false, and that dualism was after all true. Smart's reply to this is to accept that scientific claims are contingent and so open to being falsified by new evidence: but to then say that he is not claiming anything more than that the identity thesis *might* turn out in fact to be true – that no argument can be given to show that it *must* be false.

Thirdly, the objector might be willing to accept that there was no separate mental *substance*, but still want to uphold a different kind of dualism, according to which mental *properties* were irreducibly distinct in kind from physical properties. For instance, the properties of the after-image include such things as 'being yellowish-orange', which do not belong to the brain-process which is going on when someone has the image; and conversely, the brain-process has properties, like being located in a particular part of the brain, which do not belong to the after-image. But, Smart replies, we can account for this without having to say that the after-image and the brain-process are distinct things. 'Having a yellowish-orange after-image', for instance, can be analysed as meaning 'Having something going on which is like what happens when one is really seeing something yellowish-orange'. Smart, like Place, emphasizes that his claim is not that *after-images* are identical to brain-processes, but that *having* after-images is: having after-images is no more coloured or located in space than brain-processes are. This reply also works for another objection, that it makes sense to say of brain-processes but not of after-images that they are, for example, swift or slow.

Next, Smart considers the criticism that after-images are essentially *private*, accessible only to the person who has them, whereas brain-processes are *public*, observable by anyone at all who is in the appropriate position. His reply to this seems to be that this difference is due simply to the rules of language we happen to have adopted: we have decided that normally what someone says about their own after-images cannot be corrected by anyone else. The implication *seems* to be that we could always decide to adopt a different rule, say, that people's statements about their own after-images are as open to correction as their statements about their own brain-processes. If we could change our ways of talking in this way, then that would presumably show that there is no *metaphysical* distinction between after-images and brain-processes. (It should be said, however, that Smart nowhere establishes that it would be possible to change our ways of thinking in this way. Is it *just* a way of talking, or is there some sense in which it is rooted in the reality of things? Smart simply does not consider these questions.)

Next Smart considers a possible 'thought experiment' – quite a common tactic adopted by some philosophers to show what is supposed to be logically possible. In this case, the suggestion is that we could perfectly well imagine a stone statue (with no brain-processes) as having after-images and similar conscious experiences. But even if this is imaginable, and so logically possible, Smart argues, it would not show that having after-images isn't *in fact*, in the *real* world, identical with a brain-process. (He is right that this does not follow, but we might go further and doubt whether, if we really think about it, we could imagine a being made of stone as having conscious experiences: what would that really *mean*?) Smart rounds off his discussion by referring again to Wittgenstein's argument against the possibility of a private language, already examined in Chapter 1. If conscious experience were genuinely private, as the dualist theory claims, then how, Smart asks, could the language in which we talk about each other's after-images, pains and other experiences ever get established? In order for this to be possible, such talk must refer to something public and shareable, so that there could be shared criteria for saying when it was right or wrong to say 'I have a pain in my stomach' or 'I have a yellowish-orange after-image'. (Again, however, it does not follow that what we refer to must be a brain-process: indeed, it seems very unlikely that this is how we give a public reference to our talk of pains or after-images.)

The arguments which Smart discusses are not the only ones which might be used by dualists to show that science could never possibly show that conscious experiences and brain-processes are identical. But Smart's examination of them goes some way towards making it plausible that we should not be making any kind of philosophical mistake if we were led by the development of science to conclude that there was nothing more going on when, for instance, we have a yellowish-orange after-image than certain processes in our brain and nervous system. The only question that remains for both Place and Smart, and it is crucial, is whether this shows that conscious experiences and brain-processes are 'contingently identical'.

At the heart of this whole issue is the question of what exactly we *mean* by saying that one thing is 'identical with' another – that they are not two things which are correlated with each other, but are in fact one and the same. One much-discussed recent philosopher who has considered this issue, partly in connection with the mind–brain problem, is Saul Kripke (see especially Kripke 1980). Kripke accepts that some statements of identity are indeed contingent: an example he gives is 'The man who invented bifocals was the first Postmaster General of the United States'. Both the two descriptions which are used in this sentence in fact refer to Benjamin Franklin, so it is a true identity statement. But it might not have been true: Benjamin Franklin might not have invented bifocals, or might not have been the first US Postmaster General. So it is a *contingently* true identity statement, and it is also one which we have discovered to be true by empirical historical research, not one we could have seen to be true *a priori* (like, say, '6 = 3 × 2'). But Kripke argues that it is a mistake to think that it follows that any identity statement which is discovered to be true empirically is therefore contingent.

In arguing for this, Kripke starts from a conviction that there is a difference between referring to something by describing some property which it has and directly naming it. It is, he accepts, a contingent or chance matter that a particular description applies to a particular object (as in the example given, the description 'inventor of bifocals' might not have been true of the same person as the description 'First Postmaster General of the United States'). But it is not, and cannot be, a contingent matter, he says, that an object is the same as itself: so that saying that 'A = B', where 'A' and 'B' are two different names for the same object, must be stating a *necessary* truth, one that cannot be false no matter what.

There is an old philosophical way of characterizing necessary truth: a statement expresses a necessary truth when it is 'true in all possible worlds', that is, would still be true no matter how the world might be changed. For example, 'a triangle has three sides' is true in all possible worlds (or at least in all worlds where there are triangles), because it is part of the *essence* of a triangle, part of what makes something a triangle, that it is a three-sided plane figure. Thus, no matter how the world might be changed, there could not be a world in which there were, say, four-sided triangles. But the statement that the triangle which a particular geometry teacher is pointing to in his lesson is drawn in chalk on a blackboard is not necessarily true: the teacher might have drawn it with a pen on paper, or might not even have drawn it at all: it is perfectly easy to conceive of the world as being different in this way. Having said that, we can now introduce a technical term which Kripke uses: 'rigid designator'. A rigid designator is an expression which identifies an object in terms of its essence (as 'triangle' does), rather than in terms of some description which just happens to be true of it (as 'the figure drawn in chalk on the blackboard by Mr Smith' does). Hence, a rigid designator identifies the same object in any possible world: if 'A' and 'B' are both rigid designators of a certain object, then 'A = B' is a statement of *necessary*, not *contingent*, identity.

How is all this related to the mind–body question? The identity theorists, Kripke assumes, argue that conscious states, such as pain, are contingently identical to brain states or processes, such as the firing of certain neurons, much in the same way that lightning is contingently identical to electrical discharges in the atmosphere, or (to use one of Kripke's own examples) that heat is identical to the motion of molecules. The latter cases are supposed to be contingent identities because we needed scientific research to discover them, and the mind–brain identity is supposed to be contingent as something which it is assumed will be shown by future scientific research. But, Kripke argues, this is mistaken on two counts. First, 'heat is the motion of molecules', if true at all, is *necessarily* true, true in all possible worlds, because 'heat' and 'the motion of molecules' are rigid designators. It is of the essence of heat that it should be the motion of molecules, and the fact that it required scientific research on our part to discover that essence does not alter things in the slightest: there could not be heat without the motion of molecules and vice versa. (There could of course be the motion of molecules without our *feeling* hot, but the ability to cause feelings of heat in animals of a certain kind is not part of the essence of what it is referred to scientifically as heat.) Second, the way in which these [i.e. statements like 'Heat is the motion of molecules'] have turned out to be necessary truths does not seem to me to be a way in which the mind–brain identities could turn out to be either necessary or contingently true.

(Kripke 1980: 99 ff.)

Like 'heat' and 'molecular motion', Kripke argues, 'pain' and 'the firing of certain neurons' are both rigid designators. 'Can any case of essence', he asks, 'be more obvious than the fact that *being a pain* is a necessary property of each pain?' (Kripke 1980: 146). It may sound at first as if Kripke were merely referring to the tautology 'A pain is (necessarily) a pain'; but the point he is making is subtler. He is saying that there is only one way in which we can identify something as a pain, in any possible world, namely, by its painfulness. Unless it had this essential feature, it would no more be a pain than a four-sided figure would be a triangle. But the same is true, he says, of the associated brain state (call it 'B'):

not only being a brain state, but even being a brain state of a specific type is an essential property of *B*. The configuration of brain cells whose presence at any given time constitutes the presence of *B* at that time is essential to *B*, and in its absence *B* would not have existed.

(Kripke 1980: 147)

In any possible world in which *B* existed, according to Kripke, there would have to be that particular configuration of cells.

If Kripke is right, therefore, the statement 'Pain is a particular configuration of brain cells' would have, if true, to be *necessarily* so: it would be inconceivable that there could be a pain without that configuration of brain cells, and that there could be that configuration of brain cells without pain. But it is clearly not inconceivable. To be in pain is to have a certain unpleasant sensation, and there is nothing in the nature of having that pain that requires that the brain should be in any state at all, let alone in any particular state. Equally, being in state *B* can be identified simply in terms of the particular configuration of cells involved, without any reference to sensations of pain: presumably, a corpse, which has no sensations at all, (or an anaesthetized living person) could for instance still have a brain in state *B*. So even if scientific progress were to establish that whenever we feel pain, our brains are always as a matter of fact in state B, that would not establish that being in pain and being in brain-state B were *identical*, one and the same thing. A Cartesian dualist could perfectly well accept, as we have seen, that there was a regular correlation between states of consciousness and brain states, but that in itself would not lead to the conclusion that states of consciousness were nothing more than brain states.

IV

Even if we accept Kripke's argument as far as it goes, however, we may still feel that the problem has not been disposed of. Part of the strength of materialism, as Kripke himself recognizes, is that it attempts to avoid what were earlier called 'nomological danglers' – phenomena which cannot be fitted into the general laws of science and seem to require special ad hoc laws of their own. This is really just another way of stating one of the primary difficulties with Cartesian dualism, stated in Chapter 1. Even if Descartes is perfectly within his rights, logically speaking, to accept a parallelism between brain states and states of consciousness, there is still the problem of how he is to account for this parallelism. He might (as some much more recent philosophers have in effect done) simply accept it as a brute fact, a mystery which we can never adequately resolve. But that seems hardly satisfactory from a scientific point of view, especially in view of the constantly increasing growth of detailed neuroscientific knowledge about the parallels. Perhaps, however, we can reformulate materialism in such a way that it will both avoid Kripkean objections and also still be able to offer better answers than Descartes could to the problems of interaction.

The identity thesis is a *reductionist* theory: that is, it attempts to show that the study of human mental life (psychology, for short) can ultimately be seen to be a branch of a more fundamental science, in this case, neurophysiology. To say that it is a 'branch' means that the laws of psychology can themselves be explained in terms of the laws of neurophysiology; or that what we are really talking about when we refer to thoughts, sensations, wishes and so on can be translated without loss of meaning into statements about processes going on in the brain. But this kind of reductionism still seems to give psychological statements some meaning of their own, and that is part of the problem which gives rise to the Kripkean objections. (The meaning of 'pain' seems to be different from that of 'firing of certain neurons'). This has suggested that what materialists need is not reductionism, but something much more radical: the actual *elimination* of any separate science of psychology, or any idea that we are talking about anything real when we use terms like 'thought', 'wish', 'pain' and so on, rather than terms like 'firings of certain neurons'. This more radical view is normally called 'eliminative materialism' or 'eliminativism' for short.

Two of the most determined advocates of eliminative materialism are Paul and Patricia Churchland. Among their numerous papers and books, some written jointly and some by each of them individually, one paper by Paul Churchland called 'Eliminative materialism and the propositional attitudes' (Churchland 2004) is particularly often cited, since it is a very clear and concise statement of what eliminative materialism is and what the principal arguments in its favour are. The article begins with a definition:

> Eliminative materialism is the thesis that our common-sense conception of psychological phenomena constitutes a radically false theory, a theory so fundamentally defective that both the principles and the ontology of that theory will eventually be displaced, rather than smoothly reduced, by completed neuroscience.
>
> (Churchland 2004: 382)

The last few words of this definition are important. Like the identity theorists, eliminativists look to the advance of neuroscience to rid us of our dualistic hang-ups, our traditional belief that we have a non-physical soul. This will come to seem as superstitious, materialists think, as the belief that lightning and thunder express the anger of the gods, rather than simply electrical activity in the atmosphere. But whereas identity theorists still want to go on talking about states of consciousness, while identifying them with something material, namely, states of the brain, eliminative materialists simply say that 'consciousness talk' represents an outmoded and useless theory for explaining human behaviour, and needs to be replaced by a new and better way of explaining it which will use only the vocabulary and concepts of neuroscience. Instead of trying to *identify* pain with the firing of C-fibres, and so getting into all the Kripkean difficulties about identity, we should simply drop the talk of pain altogether, and *only* talk about the firing of C-fibres (or whatever other concept a 'completed neuroscience' comes up with to explain what happens when human beings suffer injury and start crying out, writhing about and so on).

This involves thinking of our 'common-sense conception of psychological phenomena' as trying to do the same kind of thing as the theories of neuroscience, but not doing it anything like so well. Many, perhaps most, people would find this comparison unconvincing. We do not normally think of our common-sense explanations of our own and other people's behaviour as some kind of primitive scientific theory, but just as 'common sense': that is, as embodying what we all instinctively understand, without the need for specialist scientific study, just through being human.

Hence, one of the first things the eliminativist must try to do is to show that common-sense ways of understanding human behaviour are just a network of concepts which functions in the same way as any other empirical theory. It seems like plain common sense, the eliminativist says, only because it has been taken for granted for so long: but being taken for granted for a long time is not by any means a guarantee that a theory is correct. Churchland compares common-sense psychology, or 'folk psychology' as he likes to call it, to the view which used to be held before the rise of modern physics at the time of Galileo and which one could call similarly 'folk physics'. According to folk physics, for example, things have natural tendencies (tendencies which are part of their nature) to move in certain directions: stones fall downwards, towards the earth, because that is the nature of such things; flames move upwards, because that is their nature. The facts described are true, and these generalizations provide perfectly reliable means of predicting what will happen if you let go of a stone or light a fire. But modern physics has made progress in understanding matter in motion on a much wider scale by replacing all such talk of natural directions of motion by, for example, Newton's laws of gravitational attraction, which apply equally to stones, flames, planets, space ships and any other kind of physical object.

In the same way, Churchland argues, we should now look on folk psychology as a theory on the way out. It certainly, he admits, allows us most of the time to predict each other's behaviour in everyday situations with remarkable success. But the very fact that it does so shows that it works like a scientific theory, which formulates generalizations, or laws, from which predictions can be derived. And so, like any other theory, it can be superseded by another theory which formulates better laws which enable us to make more successful and more wide-ranging predictions. Folk psychology, in Churchland's view, falls short in many ways, such as the nature and function of sleep, or what he describes as 'the miracle of memory, with its lightning capacity for relevant retrieval'. He gives most prominence, however, to three particular examples. It leaves largely mysterious, first, the nature and dynamics of mental illness; secondly, creative imagination; and thirdly, the differences in intelligence between different individuals. (In Chapter 6, we shall come back to these examples and reconsider them in the light of our later discussion.)

The distinctive thing about folk psychology, Churchland argues, is that it makes use of the idea of *intentionality*. More will be said in the next chapter about intentionality, but something needs to be said briefly here, in order to explain Churchland's point. Folk psychology makes use of concepts like 'thought', 'feeling', 'wish', 'hope' and so on. For instance someone is said to have acted in a certain way because she thought she could achieve her ends that way, or because she felt upset about something, or wished to have something, or hoped for a certain response. All these concepts are 'intentionalistic', in the sense that they are *directed towards a certain object, which may or may not actually exist*. A thought or a feeling is a thought or feeling *about* something, a wish or a hope is a wish or a hope *for* something, and so on. The something I am, say, thinking about may or may not actually exist: I may think, for instance, either about my son who does actually exist, or about the daughter I never had. It is this direction towards particular objects, rather than any internal characteristics, which defines a thought or other intentionalistic entity, which differentiates, for example, one thought from another.

The concepts of neuroscience, like those of most modern sciences, are not intentionalistic in this sense. A particular set of brain cells, just as such, is distinguished from another set simply by the internal characteristics of each: what cells it includes, where they are in the brain, what their pattern of electrical activity is and so on. Furthermore, what immediately causes a particular set of brain cells to behave in a certain way must be some actually existing object or state of affairs in the brain, which behaves in an appropriate way at an earlier time. That is why folk psychology cannot be reduced to neuroscience: its concepts can't be translated without loss of meaning into neuroscientific concepts. But when one theory cannot be reduced to another, we have to consider which is superior from a scientific point of view. Here Churchland thinks the answer is obvious: folk psychology is far inferior, and ought therefore to be abandoned, just as alchemy was abandoned in favour of modern chemistry, or the view that the earth is the centre of everything was abandoned in favour of the view that the earth is just a planet circulating the sun.

He gives a number of reasons for this. First, there are the numerous phenomena mentioned above which folk psychology, according to him, simply fails to explain. These failures show 'decisively', Churchland claims, that 'FP [folk psychology] is *at best* a highly superficial theory, a partial and unpenetrating gloss on a deeper and more complex reality' (Churchland 2004: 388). Secondly, folk psychology is 'stagnant and infertile': that is, it is not continually increasing its power to explain, as a living scientific theory ought to. We are not really any better, he says, at explaining human behaviour in its terms than the ancient Greeks were. Thirdly, unlike neuroscience, it does not fit in with the ways of thinking characteristic of physical science generally. This is the point which we have considered before about 'nomological danglers'. Neuroscience uses the same kind of concepts as other physical sciences, and so coheres with them as part of a unified scientific account of the world, including ourselves. For example, it explains human behaviour in terms of electro-chemical processes in the brain, which links human behaviour to the general theory of electricity, and so ultimately to fundamental physical and chemical principles. Folk psychology, with its intentionalistic concepts, has a way of explaining human behaviour which simply does not belong in such a unified scientific picture: it is, in the term which Churchland takes over from the philosophy of science, 'incommensurable' with the categories of physical science. The physical sciences do not explain phenomena in terms of intentionalistic concepts: the rainbow, for instance, does not appear in the sky because someone wants it to be there, but simply because light happens to be diffracted through raindrops.

Eliminative materialism is thus the view, not that thoughts, feelings and sensations are identical with brain-processes, but that we should stop talking (at least for scientific purposes) about thoughts, feelings and sensations, and talk only about states and processes in the brain and nervous system. This would give us a wholly different, and, Churchland argues, a much more fruitful, way of explaining human behaviour, and one which belonged in a unified scientific view of the world. So this is not just a scientific claim, like the claim that one theory in neuroscience is better than another: such a scientific claim could be supported or refuted by experimental evidence. The eliminativist claim is a *metaphysical* one, about the whole way in which we see reality, and about what reality contains (as Churchland himself says, it is about 'ontology', the philosophical theory of 'what there is'). Eliminativists are in effect saying that there are no such things as thoughts, feelings, sensations, etc.; that all there really are are neurons, neurotransmitters, electrical currents and other physical or material things. It is supposed to be like saying that there are really no such things as ghosts, only tricks of the light which deceive nervous people in certain situations. In both cases, empirical evidence cannot prove or disprove the claim in any direct way, since it depends on a particular way of *interpreting* the empirical data. But it can be argued (and this is essentially how Churchland argues), that, if one way of interpreting the data explains them in a way which is more fruitful and more consistent with the rest of science, then that is a reason for accepting it.

V

Are there any objections to eliminativism which do not depend on a general opposition to a scientific view of the world? A number of criticisms deserve consideration. One kind of criticism comes from an alternative philosophical view of the nature of mental concepts which has had a significant following in recent philosophy: this is the view called 'functionalism'. In order to make its criticism of eliminativism more understandable, and also for its own sake, we shall need to say something at this stage about what functionalism is. (Though we must bear in mind that, as functionalists themselves would accept, there are several versions of what it is which do not always exactly coincide with each other.) The essential idea of functionalism is that when we talk about 'thoughts', 'feelings', 'sensations' and the like, we are not talking about things made of a certain kind of 'stuff' (spiritual stuff or material stuff) but of 'the causal role of the particular in the mental life of the organism' (Fodor 2004: 174). To take a simple example: 'pain', for a functionalist, is defined, not as something which happens in the soul or in the nervous system, but as something which is caused by such things as injury to the body and which causes the person or animal affected to do things like crying out, withdrawing the affected part from contact with what is damaging it, and tending to avoid contact with things of the harmful type.

In this sense, functionalism is compatible with either Cartesian dualism or materialism, or indeed with any other theory of what happens when we suffer pain. On the functionalist account, a being of any type – a computer, or robot or Martian, say – which was constructed very differently from human beings or other living earth creatures could still feel pain, as long as there was something which played that causal role in its life. As Fodor points out in the article just cited, functionalism arose through reflection on such things as Artificial Intelligence, computation theory and cybernetics. Partly for that reason, it is often expressed by means of a metaphor derived from computers, that mental life belongs to the 'software' rather than the 'hardware' – that it is like a computer program which can be realized in computers of very different physical construction.

There is nothing in functionalism, to repeat, which actually rules out materialism as such. A functionalist could perfectly consistently accept a materialist metaphysics, according to which there was no such thing as Descartes's 'mental substance', but only physical things (things of the kind talked about in physics). Some functionalists, such as Shoemaker, would even say that functionalism *implies* that mental terms can in principle be eliminated. But most functionalists would deny that, for a reason which Churchland discusses in his article. Talk about thoughts, feelings, etc., can't, they would say, be eliminated even in principle, because it is part of the way in which we *evaluate* human behaviour as 'rational' or 'irrational' (this is what Churchland refers to as the 'normative' character of folk psychology). Suppose, for example, someone suffers from the delusion that he is Napoleon: we characterize this as a 'delusion' because we regard it as an irrational belief. That is, it is a belief for which he does not have sufficient evidence of the right kind. Indeed, he holds on to it in the face of overwhelming contrary evidence (he does not live in France, but in Britain, his mother tongue is English, not French, he lives in the twenty-first century, not in the eighteenth and nineteenth, and so on and so forth).

We can call this person's behaviour irrational to the extent that it results from an irrational belief: but the term 'irrational', while it can be applied to things like beliefs, cannot be meaningfully used of things like the firing of neurons. So, the argument goes, as long as we need to make such distinctions, we cannot do without folk psychology or replace it by neuroscience, since we cannot do without such folk-psychological concepts as 'belief' in making and explaining the distinction. The philosopher Hilary Putnam, as Churchland says, has argued that folk psychology cannot therefore be treated as a falsifiable scientific theory in the way that eliminativists suggest. However, Churchland vigorously rejects this functionalist argument as 'a smokescreen for the preservation of error and confusion' (Churchland 2004: 393). He compares it to the attempt to defend alchemy against modern chemistry by pointing to the alleged functional role of alchemical concepts and explanations. Surely, he asks, it is not the intentionalistic character of the concepts of folk psychology which makes it possible to evaluate human cognitive behaviour in these ways. The eliminative materialist can accept that some ways of responding to the world around us are more 'rational' than others – more efficient, for example, in satisfying our needs. But, he implies, we do not need to use intentionalistic concepts in describing what makes them more rational.

> Eliminative materialism thus does not imply the end of our normative concerns. It implies only that they will have to be reconstituted at a more revealing level of understanding, the level that a matured neuroscience will provide.
>
> (Churchland 2004: 395)

All this, however, is very vague: it is never spelled out in any detail just *how* a 'matured neuroscience' will enable us to make our normative distinctions without using intentionalistic concepts like thought, belief, wish, hope and so on. We are simply supposed to take it on trust, and there are very good reasons for not doing so. Let us go back again to the man who believes he is Napoleon. His consequent behaviour might include such things as wearing Napoleonic uniform, being very imperious in his dealings with other people, expressing regret about 'his' defeat at Waterloo and so on. Is any of these modes of behaviour irrational in the sense of being an inefficient way of securing his *objective* needs (such as the need for food, sleep or sex)? Not necessarily: indeed, it might be that his behaviour persuaded other people, maybe through fear, to provide him with food and sex. If his behaviour is crazy, as it clearly is, it is because it results from a crazy *belief*, and belief is an essentially intentionalistic concept: we can distinguish one belief from another only in virtue of *what* it is which is believed. It is difficult to see how his crazy belief that he is Napoleon could be distinguished in purely neurological terms from Buonaparte's own, perfectly reasonable, belief about his identity. Whatever processes in the brain are involved in believing 'I am Napoleon' (or 'Je suis Napoléon') must presumably be the same whether or not the belief is irrational. Even the thought-processes which led to the belief in the two cases can be distinguished only by using such terms as 'logical' and 'illogical', and these terms are not part of the vocabulary of neuroscience as such. So we cannot account for his delusion in terms of the concepts of neuroscience, however 'complete'.

But this is a criticism which could equally well be applied to functionalism, at least as Fodor defines it. If mentalistic terms like 'thought' or 'belief' are to be defined in terms of their causal role – what causes them and what they cause – then does that make it any easier to use normative terms like 'rational' in application to them than to Churchland's neuron-firings? To describe someone's belief as 'rational' or 'irrational' is to apply certain human standards of rationality to it, not to describe what caused the believer to hold it, or what effects their holding of it may have. To say that someone's belief is 'irrational' is to say that they have deviated from these standards, in a situation in which they might have been expected to recognize and follow them.

This is a way in which human mental operations are not like computer programs. Computers may sometimes be called 'logic machines', but they do not really act logically: the conclusions they arrive at may logically follow from the premises *in human eyes*, but the computers themselves are not even trying to obey the rules of logic, just behaving as the program causes them to do. Furthermore, even although functionalism in this sense is not necessarily 'material-ist', in the sense of saying that minds are made of material stuff, it does imply that minds must be realized in *some* kind of stuff. And this stuff is very likely to be material in some way. Computer programs are in fact realized in some kind of material hardware, even if it may take variable forms; and if mental operations are to be defined in terms of their 'causal roles', then there could be just the same arguments from the need for a unified science for saying that that implies that the hardware of thought must be made of the same matter as is studied in physics and chemistry.

An alternative line of defence for the eliminativist would be to say, as Churchland does, that we should make the effort to abstract from the use of folk psychological ways of talking as part of our everyday transactions with each other, since that obscures its failings in more theoretical areas (see Churchland 2004: 389). We could expand this point by saying that, while folk psychology may have its uses in everyday life – for example, in allowing us to make distinctions between rational and irrational beliefs and behaviour – that does not make it a true account of human beings and their behaviour: for that, we must turn to neuroscience. This brings us to the heart of the whole issue about the various forms of materialism. As has been repeated throughout this chapter, materialism is ultimately motivated by the assumption that only science, and science understood in a certain way, can tell us the ultimate truth about ourselves and our place in the world. It is that assumption which needs to be questioned if we are to really see what might be wrong with classical materialism.

SUBJECTIVITY, INTENTIONALITY
AND BEHAVIOUR

I

In the first two chapters, we have considered some philosophical accounts of mind which are based on the assumption that 'mind' is the name of a *thing* or 'substance'. If we make that assumption, the question of what it is to have a mind becomes one of what *kind* of substance it is, what this thing called 'mind' is made of. It can be seen as a unique kind of thing, utterly different from anything material or physical, as in Cartesian dualism. Or it can be regarded as a thing just like anything else, something which is part of the physical universe and governed by the laws of physical science, as in classical materialism. But the difficulties we have seen in both dualism and classical materialism suggest that this whole approach may be misguided. Maybe we should go back a step and reconsider the whole issue from a different point of view. Instead of thinking of the question 'What is mind?' as something like the question 'What is gold?', to be answered by developing a theory of its essential nature, it might be better to ask first what we mean when we talk about people's mental lives, or that they have minds as well as bodies. We mean, of course, that they are capable of such things as thought, feeling and sensation, as well as of such things as breathing, digesting and walking. Then we can ask whether these 'mental' activities and states have special, characteristic features of their own which make them different in some important way from 'physical' or 'bodily' activities and states. This approach changes the focus of our thinking about minds: we now concentrate on the beings who 'have' minds, and on the role which the 'mental' plays in their lives in general, rather than on what kind of substance or 'stuff' minds are made of.

Descartes, as we saw, thought that what was essential to the mental was *consciousness*: what is mental is conscious and unextended, what is material is extended and unconscious. A thought, for example, is not extended: that is, it does not occupy any space, it has no spatial dimensions and no position in space. Where is my thought that Descartes believed this? It might be said that it is in my head: but where in my head? We could not open up my skull and discover my thought about Descartes (though we could probably discover the part of my brain which is active when I am having thoughts). And, as we saw in Chapter 1, it makes little sense to ask how many centimetres long my thought about Descartes is (whereas we can ask how long a particular set of neurons is). Saying my thought is 'in my head' seems to be simply a metaphorical way of saying that I am thinking it, or that my brain is active when I am thinking it.

More positively, Descartes says that my thought is 'conscious': that is, that when I think it, I know, without having to infer it, that I am having this thought. If someone asked me 'What are you thinking about just now?', I could immediately answer 'I'm thinking about Descartes's view of the essence of mind'. As was argued in Chapter 1, we could object to Descartes's view on the grounds that we can have *un*conscious thoughts, emotions, wishes, etc. But perhaps if we reflect a little about what is meant by being 'conscious', we could arrive at a wider view of what is characteristic of the mental, which would include but go beyond Descartes's definition.

What is it about thought (to stick with that example) which makes it possible for thoughts to be conscious in the sense just defined? I can know what I am thinking because I am the one thinking it: I can't know what you are thinking unless you choose to tell me. Each of us has his or her own thoughts, to which we alone can have *direct* access in this sense. Others can, of course, have less direct access, by for instance asking us what we are thinking, or inferring our thoughts from our outward behaviour or some other form of evidence. And there can be thoughts of mine to which I don't currently have any access at all, and thus others may be able in these cases to know better, by indirect means, what I am thinking than I do myself. None of this is inconsistent with the important point that I alone can have *direct* access to my thoughts (and wishes, and emotions, and desires, and other mental states and activities). In this sense, my own mental life is very definitely *mine*, not something which is shared with others. Importantly, only I can have my thoughts, and I can't have your thoughts: this is part of what we mean by the word 'thought'. We can call this the 'subjectivity' of the mental. I am the *subject* of my own mental life – *I* am the person who has these thoughts, feelings, wishes, etc.; and no mental life can exist which is not *someone's* mental life – there cannot be a thought without a thinker, a subject. Subjectivity includes consciousness in Descartes's sense, but goes beyond it: a thought can still be subjective, even if it is not conscious.

The idea of consciousness has been linked to another idea, which was discussed fairly briefly in the previous chapter, that of *intentionality*. To say that thoughts, emotions and so on are conscious is to say that they are thoughts *of* something, feelings *about* something, etc. It would make no sense to say that someone was, for instance, thinking, but not thinking *about* anything. There is a movement in philosophy called 'phenomenology' (to be discussed in more detail later in the chapter). One of the central tenets of phenomenology is that consciousness is intentional, expressed in the slogan that all consciousness is consciousness *of something*. What that implies, given what was said in the last chapter about intentionality, is that to say that someone is conscious is to say something about that person's relation to some object of which they are conscious. It was the nineteenth-century Austrian philosopher Franz Brentano who re-introduced the medieval term 'intentionality' to describe this essential relatedness of consciousness to an object. In his *Psychology from an Empirical Standpoint*, he explains the term 'intentionality' by calling it 'reference to a content, direction toward an object (which is not to be understood here as meaning a thing), or immanent objectivity' (see Brentano, in Moran and Mooney (eds) 2002: 41). A thought is essentially *about something*, and we can distinguish one thought from another only by distinguishing what they are about (their 'intentional objects'): thus, a thought about Descartes is a different thought from one about Paul Churchland. In this sense, the intentional object is 'immanent' in the thought, part of the thought, part of what makes it the thought it is. But, as Brentano says, the intentional object need not be a 'thing'. It can be a quality, or a state of affairs, or anything else that one can meaningfully think about: the intentional object of my thought might not be a thing, like a rose, but the smell of the rose, or the beautiful arrangement of the roses in the garland. And, very importantly, as was mentioned in the last chapter, the intentional object of my thought need not be something which actually exists, or a state of affairs which is actually the case: I can think about abstractions, which do not actually exist, or about the past, which no longer exists, or about mythological beings who never existed and never will do. (And of course, what is said here about thoughts also goes, with relevant changes, for other mental acts and states like feelings, desires, wishes, hopes, motives and so on).

Two questions arise about Brentano's account of intentionality. First, is it really true that *every* form of consciousness must be intentional? One obvious example which doesn't seem to fit is pain or sensations in general. Being in pain is a conscious state: if someone is in pain, they know immediately that they are. But pains do not seem to be *about* some object: they just *are*. Putting it differently, we distinguish one pain from another by its internal features – its intensity, its location and so on, not by any relation to an object. So that seems to imply that we need to limit the scope of Brentano's account – not everything which is conscious is intentional. Many philosophers, interestingly, in giving an example of something 'mental', tend to concentrate on pain sensations (and there have been several examples of that in this book already). But if we look at ordinary, non-philosophical, talk about people's minds, this does not seem such an obvious example. We think of pains as 'mental' in a sense – they are conscious, as we said, and they are certainly subjective: there couldn't be a pain which was not *someone's* pain, and my pain is necessarily different from yours. But they do not seem to be central to what we think of as 'mental'.

Another example which comes closer to the heart of what we mean by the 'mental' is moods, such as depression, euphoria, boredom and so on. The problem here is slightly different. If we are depressed, say, then we may certainly be depressed *about* something, so in that sense depression, unlike pain, can be intentional. Sometimes, what we are depressed about is something specific: as we may be depressed about our exam results or about breaking up with someone we love. But sometimes what we are depressed about is hard to pin down. We just feel depressed and, if someone asks us what about, we may well reply, 'Oh, nothing in particular'. We might say that our depression still has an intentional object, but one which is very general – we are depressed 'about life' or 'about the world'. This sounds a little like an attempt to fit moods like depression into a general view of the mental as intentional, and so perhaps should be resisted. So perhaps the nearest we could come to Brentano and the phenomenologists is to say that intentionality is a feature of the *central core* of our mental lives, but not necessarily of more peripheral areas like sensations and moods.

This leads on to the second question. Need what is intentional be conscious? Not necessarily: an unconscious thought or feeling, after all, is still a thought or feeling about something (otherwise we couldn't really call it a 'thought' or a 'feeling'). If one of Freud's patients had an unconscious hatred of their father, it would be as intentional as a conscious hatred: whether I hate my father consciously or unconsciously, my emotion is still directed towards an intentional object, namely, my father. Unconscious hatred of my father can only be distinguished from unconscious hatred of, say, my brother because their intentional objects are different. Thus intentionality too includes consciousness and goes beyond it. The answers to these two questions, taken together with what was said earlier about subjectivity, suggest that it is a mistake to *define* the 'mental' too sharply or precisely. To say what we mean by the mental is perhaps better seen as a matter of distinguishing a central core of human attributes, activities, processes and so on to which the term applies: these would include thought, emotion, desire and the like, whose essential characteristics are subjectivity and intentionality. Then other human attributes could be called 'mental' to the extent that they are like the central core, e.g. in being subjective but not intentional.

II

Does thinking of the mental in this way make a sharp distinction between the mental and the physical or material? There could be such a distinction even if the mental and the material were made of the same kind of stuff: even if human beings are nothing but biological organisms of a certain kind, there might still be differences between at any rate the central ways in which we talk about the activities of those organisms which involved 'mind' and those which did not. For example, subjectivity and intentionality might be implied when we talked about someone thinking about his dinner, but utterly irrelevant when we talked about him digesting his dinner. This seems indeed to be so. My thought about my dinner is necessarily *my* thought, not someone else's: but the digestive process which in fact goes on in my body could be exactly the same in someone else's body if, through some complicated surgery, my gastrointestinal system were transplanted into it. So the digestive organs and processes which happen, as a matter of fact, to be mine might have been someone else's. Similarly, my thought about my dinner is essentially intentional, and that in this case implies that I have some concept of what a 'dinner' is on my part – how could I think about dinner unless I knew what 'dinner' was? But digesting dinner can be fully described without any reference to 'dinner' as an intentional object, just in terms of its internal properties. A mouse digests its dinner in exactly the same sense that a human being does.

This creates difficulties for the identity thesis version of materialism. According to that thesis, as we saw, thoughts, feelings and sensations are to be identified with brain-processes. But if thoughts and feelings have properties of subjectivity and intentionality whereas brain-processes don't, then it is to say the least difficult to see how the two kinds of things can be identified. And if sensations have subjectivity when brain-processes don't, then pains and neuron-firings can't be identical (this is of course part of Kripke's point). Of course, it is true, as Smart points out, that lightning can be said to have certain properties which electrical discharges in the atmosphere don't have – brightness, being awe-inspiring and so on, and that this does not lead us to deny that they are identical. But the difference in that case is simply one between the intrinsic properties which the electrical discharges have and the effects which they have on human perceivers. That is a different kind of difference from that between the intrinsic properties of thoughts and those of brain-processes. It is not surprising that eliminative materialists tried to avoid this problem by simply denying that the concepts of intentionality and subjectivity had any place at all in a rational account of human behaviour.

But this too creates difficulties. For certain purposes, as we saw in the previous chapter, we can't give a rational account of human behaviour *without* using the concepts of subjectivity and intentionality. If, for instance, we wish to give an explanation of why one person is an eliminativist while another is a Cartesian dualist, it will not be a satisfactory explanation to say that the first person's brain-processes were different from the second's. Knowing what is going on in their brains when they formulate their philosophical opinions does not tell us why one person has a different opinion from the other. What we need in order to understand that is some idea of their respective *reasons* for accepting the opinions that they do. Why is one person convinced by the arguments for eliminativism, while the other finds those for dualism more persuasive? For someone to be able to hold a philosophical opinion, it is necessary, as far as we know, that they have a functioning brain, in particular one which makes logical reasoning possible. But this is not sufficient: they must also *use* those reasoning powers appropriately, in understanding and assessing arguments and arriving at their own conclusions. This involves having certain standards of assessment which one applies: in that way, they are *one's own* standards, and the conclusion one comes to by using them is *one's own* – it is 'subjective' in the sense explained. And it involves having beliefs, an intentional concept: the eliminativist, for instance, has the belief that the arguments in favour of that position are stronger than those against. The intentional object of the dualist's belief is quite a different proposition, and it is that which makes the dualist's belief different from the eliminativist's.

We seem to need the concepts of subjectivity and intentionality, therefore, in talking about human behaviour from some points of view, and we do not seem to be able to identify them with features of brain-processes. These concepts therefore pose serious difficulties for both the forms of materialism we have considered. But they are also problems for Cartesian dualism. At first sight, this might seem a strange thing to say, at least about subjectivity: for surely, one might think, the whole point of Descartes's position is that our minds are subjective – that my mind is essentially different from yours, and directly accessible only to me. Nevertheless, it can be argued that Descartes's account of the subjectivity of consciousness is unsustainable. According to Descartes, my mind is accessible only to me because it is entirely distinct from anything physical, and so is not in any sense observable in the normal way by others. It is a private, inner world which is not part of the world we share with others. But in that case, what 'I' refers to, when, for example, I say that I believe that dualism is mistaken, is something that only I have access to: you do not and cannot know what 'I' refers to when I use it. But in that case, how can we distinguish my mind from your mind (the mind you refer to when *you* use 'I')? In short, we cannot distinguish different minds unless the term 'I' has a *shared* meaning, so that I can meaningfully say 'I' for you refers to a different subject than it does for me. (This is a consequence of Wittgenstein's argument against the possibility of a purely private language, referred to in the first chapter.)

Subjectivity is thus a problem, surprising though it may seem, for Descartes, just because it involves the possibility of distinguishing my thoughts, wishes, desires, purposes and so on from yours, which in turn requires that 'my' and 'your' should be terms in a language we can both share. The problem with intentionality is even clearer. To say that consciousness, or mental life more generally, is essentially intentional is to say that it is defined, not by its internal characteristics, but by its direction towards something outside itself. My thought about Peter differs from my thought about Paul because they have different intentional objects, even if the grammatical structure, or the emotional overtones or whatever, of the two thoughts are the same. But for Descartes, thought or consciousness is defined by its internal characteristics: it is something which goes on 'inside' a person, it is non-physical and so on. To find out what I am thinking about, I must look inside myself or 'introspect', as I might look inside and find that I am thinking, for example, 'What a nice person Peter is!' But doing that will only tell me what I am thinking if I know what the name 'Peter' refers to (as well as what the meanings of the other words in the sentence are). And that involves relating my thoughts to the world outside in which Peter exists, because what 'Peter' refers to is *Peter*, the man out there, not the idea of Peter which exists in my mind. Another way of expressing this would be to say that the Cartesian mind could exist even if the world outside, including Peter, did not; but then my alleged thought about Peter would not be about Peter at all: it would indeed be about an idea of Peter which existed only in my mind.

Both materialism and Cartesian dualism, in their different ways, thus have difficulty with the subjectivity and intentionality of mental life, which seem to be central features of anything which we could recognize as a mental life. This suggests that there is something radically wrong with both views. What is the flaw? We seem to be back at the point made at the very beginning of this chapter, that both dualism and materialism think of the mind as a particular kind of thing. This is what they have in common, what makes classical materialism, as a theory of mind, in a certain way parasitic on dualism. Cartesian dualism is the view that to say that human beings have minds is to say that they are made up of two substances, mental as well as material. Classical materialism simply deletes the first of these two substances, and argues that to say that human beings have a mind is simply to say that they have a brain, a particular part of the body and so a material thing. This is the shared assumption, that 'mind' names a thing, which looks to be the root of the problems which we have seen in both theories.

III

One prominent philosopher who thought in this way was Gilbert Ryle, who taught in Oxford from the twenties to the sixties of the twentieth century. In a number of books and papers, but especially in his major work *The Concept of Mind* (Ryle 1990), Ryle criticized Cartesian dualism (but also to some extent what we have called classical materialism) on the grounds that it was guilty of a 'category mistake'. He explains what he means by that term as follows: 'It represents the facts of mental life as if they belonged to one logical type or category (or range of types of categories), when they actually belong to another' (Ryle 1990: 17). Putting it at its simplest, Ryle claims that Cartesian dualism treats 'the mind' as the name of a peculiar kind of thing (as belonging to the category of things), when in fact it is a way of referring to certain kinds of properties and relations of human beings (it belongs to the category or categories of properties and relations). Cartesian dualism is described, with 'deliberate abusiveness', to use Ryle's own words, as 'The Myth of the Ghost in the Machine' (and by implication classical materialism is the equally mythical view of the machine without a ghost). That phrase is chosen because Descartes treats the mind as a strange spiritual substance (a 'ghost') which is somehow located in a body which is purely mechanical in its operations (a 'machine').

Category mistakes, according to Ryle, are typical philosophers' mistakes. They are made when we don't pay sufficient attention to the ways in which we actually talk about something, but try to remain at a purely abstract or theoretical level. In this case, philosophers are tempted to ignore the kinds of ways in which we actually *use* words like 'mind' – the ways we talk about people's minds and mental lives in ordinary contexts – and to try in a void to devise some general theory of what a mind must be like, to fit in with some preconceived ideas derived from religion or science or past philosophy. But this is misguided in Ryle's view: we all know perfectly well what we are saying when we make remarks like 'She has a very acute mind', or 'He is good at mental arithmetic', or 'I have it in mind to go to Tuscany this summer' or 'My mind is getting feebler as

I get older'. Philosophers should therefore reflect on these ordinary uses of 'mental conduct concepts', as Ryle calls them, if they really want to understand what it means to say that human beings have minds.

To see more clearly what Ryle is saying, we should look at some of his more detailed discussions of mental conduct concepts. Take 'intelligence', for instance. Intelligence is applying thought to action. If we are dualists, that must mean that intelligence involves a combination of two processes, one going on in the mental substance (thought), and one in the material or bodily substance (action). A typically Rylean example is someone playing tennis intelligently. On the dualist view, this would have to mean, roughly, first thinking about the theory of tennis and then moving one's arms and legs in appropriate ways. But there are various things which are obviously wrong with that account. One is that it would lead to the logical absurdity of what is known as an 'infinite regress'. To think about the theory of tennis is itself an action, and if it is to make one's tennis playing intelligent, it must presumably be an intelligent action. But on the dualist theory, that should mean that it is preceded by an action of thinking about the theory of thinking about the theory of tennis. The same move can be made again: we should have to think about the theory of thinking about the theory of thinking about the theory of tennis before we could be said to play tennis intelligently. Indeed, this move could be made an infinite number of times: so playing tennis intelligently would involve completing an infinite number of acts of thinking about the theory first. This is a logical absurdity: so the dualist account of intelligence can be reduced to absurdity, and must be mistaken. It would, in effect, mean that we could never act intelligently, because to do that would require us to perform this logically impossible task of completing an infinite number of prior actions.

If we follow Ryle's advice, and look instead at how we actually use terms like 'intelligent' in ordinary contexts, we can avoid this logical absurdity. We say that someone is playing tennis intelligently, not when we think they are performing certain 'mental' actions first before moving their arms and legs, but when we see them moving their arms and legs in certain ways – skilfully, so as to hit the ball at the right angle and with the right degree of force in order to score points off their opponent. In other words, what we mean by an action which shows intelligence is not a combination of two actions,

MIND: KEY CONCEPTS IN PHILOSOPHY

by his admission that our brains are machines and that our brains think. This admission needs some further examination if we are to see what force there is in the Strong AI argument. First we must ask whether our brains are machines. The term 'machines' is not easy to define: it usually refers to devices constructed by human beings to perform certain tasks, and clearly the brain is not a machine in that sense. What is presumably meant by calling the brain a machine is that its operations are governed by the same laws of physics and chemistry that govern the workings of machines in the ordinary sense. And it seems to be true to say that human brains are machines in that somewhat metaphorical sense. But just because this is a metaphor, it is misleading to draw general conclusions about whether 'machines' can think from the special case of the brain. This leads us on to a second question: *do* brains think? Brains certainly seem to be necessary for thinking: a being which didn't have a brain, and a brain of a particular kind, could not be said to think, as far as our scientific knowledge goes. But notice that it is the *being with the brain* that thinks, not the brain itself. Thinking is not a set of brain-processes, but a human activity (and perhaps an activity of other species of animals too).

The last sentence, as it stands, sounds rather dogmatic, but it is possible to put forward an argument in support of it. We need to consider what is involved in the activity of thinking (and this analysis could be extended, with appropriate changes, to other forms of mental activity, such as feeling, wishing, desiring and understanding). If someone is said to be thinking about, say, the nature of the brain, or the possibility of artificial intelligence, what are they doing? Essentially, they are considering certain propositions, which could be expressed in sentences of a particular language. Searle's thoughts about Strong AI, for instance, include such propositions as 'I do not understand Chinese simply on the basis of implementing a computer program for understanding Chinese' (here expressed in English). Searle could not be said to have this thought unless he understood what was meant by the words used in its expression. There may be thoughts which are too deep for words, but most thoughts must be expressible in language (and even the very deep thoughts can only be distinguished from vague feelings if some linguistic approximation to the content of the thought is possible). In that sense, thinking is using language.

The use of language, however, gets its meaning from the concepts shared by a whole linguistic community. Here we should go over again Wittgenstein's argument against the possibility of a purely private language, referred to already several times in this book. The use of words with meaning depends on following certain rules which say when it is correct to use the term in question and when it is not. In learning to use a word, we learn to follow these rules. For instance, if someone doesn't know what a 'book' is, we teach her by, first, showing her examples of books, and saying in each case that this is what we call a 'book'. She shows that she understands the word when she regularly identifies as books things which we also recognize as such, and does not identify as a 'book' something like a box of chocolates which looks rather like the books she has seen. If she does make that mistaken identification, we can correct her by saying, 'No, that's not a book, although it looks a bit like one – it's a box of chocolates. Books have to be things you can *read*' (or something of that kind).

For this reason, Wittgenstein argues, it is impossible for there to be a purely private language (that is, not simply a private code which someone else could in principle decipher, but a language which only one person could in principle understand). In such a language, words couldn't be said to be governed by rules, because there would be no possibility of real correction of someone who made a mistake in following the rules, and so there would be nothing which could be called a real *mistake*. In my 'private language', the word 'book' would mean just what I chose it to mean on any given occasion – sometimes a book, sometimes a box of chocolates, sometimes a joke and so on. In short, the expressions in the language would not have any meaning, and so the so-called 'language' would not be a language.

How is this relevant to thinking? If thinking involves considering propositions with meaning, then having a thought cannot be simply a matter of something going on in private within the individual, whether that something is processes in the soul or brain-processes. It seems reasonably well confirmed scientifically, as said earlier, that brain-processes must take place in order for us to have a thought: but they are not sufficient. In addition, we have to understand the meanings of the words in which our thoughts are expressed. That understanding in turn cannot be identified with certain brain-processes, because it requires interactions with other human beings in the world outside our brains. Simply put, we need to *learn* what words mean, and the process of learning requires our usage to be corrected by others. The meanings we learn are in that sense *shared* with others in our linguistic community, as part of certain purposive activities we have in that community. We can understand Searle's thought, not because we can look inside his brain to see what neurons are firing when he has it, but because we also know what is meant by 'implementing a computer program', 'understanding Chinese' and the rest. We understand them because we, as human beings, participate in a community in which these expressions are used, in pursuing certain activities with certain purposes. These are purposes which we do not necessarily have ourselves, but which can be explained to us, because they relate to purposes which we do have – implementing computer programs, for example, can be explained even to people who are not computer-literate by relating it to purposes like calculating, writing texts and so on with which they are already familiar. But if we did not share relevant purposes, even in this indirect way, we could not begin to understand the activity, or the words used as part of that activity. And it is *we*, whole human beings, not our brains on their own, which participate in the activity and have the purpose.

This is the real reason why machines (and indeed brains on their own) can't think. Machines can, as Searle rightly says, follow syntactic rules: they can order symbols in particular approved ways. But they are incapable of semantics, not because of the materials they are made of, but because they do not participate in a society, in shared activities pursued with a purpose. They do not do this because they do not have purposes of their own. Machines in the ordinary sense, as said above, are devices constructed by human beings to help human beings to achieve *their* purposes: a computer, for instance, is a device constructed by people to help them with calculating, word-processing, playing games and a host of other human purposes. The machine does not calculate: it manipulates symbols according to pre-set rules in such a way that the human user can interpret the outcome as a solution to the mathematical problem which concerns the user (but not the computer, which is not concerned by anything).

Unlike the machines which they use, people have purposes of their own. Some of these are necessary to them as living beings: as such they need, for example, to have the purpose of finding food to eat, of seeking shelter against the elements and perhaps of finding a mate with whom they can reproduce. In that sense, these are *biological* needs and their resulting purposes, and the purpose can be said to be 'inbuilt', part of their very nature as a biological organism. Other purposes are less obviously biological. Most human beings, for instance, have the purpose of forming relationships such as friendship with other human beings, which are not obviously connected with the need to stay alive or to reproduce the species: the particular form which these relationships take seems indeed to be determined by culture rather than biology. Nevertheless, human beings can have such purposes, or for that matter have a culture, only because they are biological creatures – living beings who act in certain ways and can therefore engage in shared activities with other members of their species. On these grounds, one could argue that thinking, and mind in general, can belong only to biological creatures, because only in their case, as was argued earlier, can there be purposes which are intrinsic to the existence of the being in question and so can confer meaning for that being on objects in its environment.

But what of the idea that perhaps we could one day construct machines modelled on the human brain. Wouldn't such machines at least be able to think? It would depend, if the argument above is correct, on whether the machines in question were modelled, not just on the brain, but on the human organism as a whole: only then could they be said to have purposes of their own, and so to interact in a social way with human beings or with other machines. There seems to be no logical impossibility about the idea of constructing living things in that sense out of materials other than flesh and blood. But, as was said earlier, being a machine in the relevant sense is not to do with the materials of which something is made, but of the use of the thing in question for purposes which are not its own. In that sense, these would not be machines. They would be artificial constructions, so that their intelligence would be artificial intelligence. The possibility of such forms of AI might well be worrying from a social point of view: but it would not show that machines could think.

All this takes us back to Merleau-Ponty's contention that our subjectivity is essentially embodied, that we are, as it is sometimes expressed, 'body-subjects'. What it means to be a subject, or to have a mind, cannot be separated from being a living being. But equally, being a living being of our sort is having a mind: human biology has to be understood as at least in part intentional and subjective, because our bodies are those of creatures who can relate to their world in these ways. This is why the brain is not a machine. It is not a device by which a human being achieves his or her ends, still less something which causes the human being to act in certain ways. Rather, it is an essential part of the human being, and its workings are part of the way in which that human being relates to the world and achieves his or her purposes.

CHAPTER 5

OTHER MINDS

I

I am having a conversation with a friend. I tell him a joke I have just heard, and he smiles broadly: one of the things which make us friends is a shared sense of humour. He then tells me how disgusted he feels about the way a colleague has been treated, and I sympathize. We talk about our plans for a meeting we are organizing, and both he and I make suggestions for some of the arrangements. Finally, we say goodbye and fix a time for seeing each other again.

This kind of conversation is a very normal feature of human life. It depends, of course, on each party understanding what the other is saying: my friend shows by his smile that he has got the point of the joke, and sees it as funny just as I do. My sympathy with what he says about his colleague's treatment in turn shows him that I know how he feels, and share his feelings. And our discussion of the plans for the meeting is clearly only possible if we each understand the other's suggestions. In all these ways, we 'know each other's mind', and if we did not, we could hardly have a conversation such as this. How is this possible? As we saw in an earlier chapter, each person is a different subject: his sense of humour, his feelings of disgust, his ideas about the meeting, are not mine, and vice versa. In order for either of us to communicate his thoughts and feelings to the other, we have to express them in some outward form, perceptible to the other: as his smile expresses his amusement, and his words, and perhaps his body-language, express his feelings of disgust. Would it perhaps be better to say, not that we 'know' each other's mind, but that we make an *informed guess* about what the other is thinking and feeling, based on these outward expressions? This would be rather like basing a scientific hypothesis on the evidence provided by the expressions: indeed, psychologists often talk about most of us as having a 'theory of mind', encoded in the brain, which enables us to decipher other people's thoughts and feelings. It certainly sometimes feels like guesswork when we are dealing with someone we don't know very well, especially if they belong to a different culture. Perhaps it only seems more certain when we are dealing with more familiar people because our experience of them helps us to pick up the signs more quickly.

This is certainly what one would think if one accepted Cartesian dualism. For Descartes, as we saw, mind and body are separate and independent substances. What goes on in the mind is therefore different from anything that goes on in the body. Thus, my thoughts and feelings are necessarily distinct from the spoken words, facial and other bodily gestures, and so on which express them. I have direct and immediate access to my thoughts and feelings – they are 'inside' me: but others have to infer what I am thinking and feeling from my outward expressions, as I have to do with theirs. Thus, knowing what someone else is thinking or feeling is always a matter of inference: I hear my friend's words saying, perhaps, 'Shall we have a drink together next Friday?' – or rather, I hear sounds issuing from my friend's mouth which sound like the sounds I should utter if I wanted to express that meaning. Then I have to infer that he means the same by those words as I would do. Maybe in his case I make that inference very quickly, so that it hardly feels like an inference: if he were a foreign visitor who spoke these words in a language I knew slightly but wasn't very familiar with, it might be more obvious, perhaps, that I was engaged in an inference.

This makes it sound as if the situation was rather like that in which I am driving at night and see a bright light coming from over the brow of a hill in front of me. I infer that these are the headlights of an oncoming vehicle. I may of course be proved wrong: when I drive further, I may see that the light is in fact coming from a floodlight in someone's garden beside the road. If someone makes an inference, they can always make it *wrongly*: perhaps, as in this case, the evidence is not enough to justify coming to the conclusion I do arrive at. But the important thing is that it ought to be possible, in principle at least, for the inferrer to discover the mistake by discovering evidence against the conclusion (as I do in this example – I see the actual source of the light). If knowing someone else's mind is making the same kind of inference as the one just referred to, then parallel things could be said about it. First of all, it must be possible for the inference to be mistaken. It certainly could be: I might take my friend's facial expression to indicate his amusement at my joke, whereas really what looked like a smile of amusement might be a pretence. He might really be smiling to be polite and to conceal his irritation at my feeble attempts at humour. But then we must ask whether, and if so how, I could discover that I'd made a mistake. If we haven't done any philosophy, and in particular if we haven't read anything by Descartes or someone in his tradition, we should say that we could, by simply observing his subsequent behaviour. If his smile looked a bit strained, I might begin to suspect that he didn't think the joke was all that good. If later on, he smiled less and showed irritation more than previously when I made a would-be funny remark, it might become clearer and clearer that we did not any longer share the same sense of humour.

But a dualist could not admit that this was a way we could discover mistakes in how we 'read' other people's minds. The dualist can certainly accept that we can be mistaken in our inferences: what my friend is thinking is a matter of fact, so that any statement I make about it can be false as well as true. But what dualists could not agree, consistently with their theory, is that we could discover our mistakes by observing later behaviour. How could that be evidence either way, since behavioural expressions are different things altogether from thoughts and feelings? Future behaviour can only be evidence for future behaviour, and we can find no stronger support in it for our hypotheses about my friend's present state of mind than we can find in his present behaviour. The whole problem of 'other minds' (to give it its traditional title) for the Cartesian is that *no* observable behaviour is or can be any kind of evidence for what is going on in someone's mind, since what is going on in another's mind is accessible only to that person.

This is uncomfortable for the dualist, since it implies that no one else can ever really *know* what someone is thinking or feeling: at best they can make an unsupported guess, which they have no means of checking. Some Cartesians have tried to avoid this discomfort by saying that we can reason here 'by analogy'. Roughly, this 'argument from analogy' goes like this: I know that, in my own case, when I smile like that, I am amused. He is smiling like that. Therefore, by analogy with my own case, I can infer that he is amused. But there are several problems in this kind of analogical reasoning. Some are immediately obvious: for instance, I know from my own case that I too do not always express amusement when I smile like this, since I too am capable of smiling insincerely. There is also a question about what exactly it means to talk of smiling 'like this': does it mean simply configuring one's mouth and face in this pattern – in which case, we haven't allowed for the different ways in which people smile? Or does it mean smiling an *amused* smile, in which case we can recognize someone's smile as one 'like this' only when we have already inferred correctly what is going on in their mind, which is viciously circular?

But the most obvious objection to reasoning by analogy is that, if Descartes is right, we have no justification for drawing the analogy. How do I know that the connection between feeling amused and smiling which holds in my case must hold in my friend's, or anyone else's, case? I can have no *independent* evidence for this, as I can in more standard cases of inference. In the motoring example, I make my inference confidently because I have known many other cases in which a light appearing over the brow of a hill came from the head-lights of an approaching car. The pattern is well established, and has been confirmed by subsequent observation. In the example, my inference was *disconfirmed* by contrary evidence, but evidence of the same kind. None of this holds in the other minds case. According to the dualist, I could not ever get inside anyone else's mind to see whether the connection between smiling and amusement holds there as well as in my own case, or to check whether I had got the inference right in this particular instance. It is almost like someone who has only ever had one experience of seeing an approaching car's head-lights coming over a hill, who sees a light over the brow of a hill and infers that it is caused by an oncoming car, but never gets the opportunity to test his inference (perhaps he turns off on to a side road before reaching the brow of the hill himself).

It might be thought that materialism, and in particular behaviour-ism, could avoid this problem, since it rejects the idea that the mind is an unobservable non-physical substance. But the various forms of materialism face a different sort of problem. The outward behaviour of someone else, in the sense of the simple physical movements of their body, is certainly as observable as my own: but if, as has been argued earlier, it is not to be equated with thoughts, feelings, sensations and so on, this will not help us to know the other person's 'mind' any better. For the same reason, the fact that we can (with the aid of instruments) observe other people's brain-processes will not help us to know their thoughts and feelings any better if, as has also been argued, brain-processes and thoughts, etc., cannot be identified with each other. All forms of materialism have difficulties with the subjectivity of mental life, and it is that subjectivity which creates the problem of knowledge of other minds.

II

So, if Descartes is right, no one can ever be sure that he has read someone else's mind correctly from that person's outward behaviour. But there is another, even more serious consequence. We can be sure that *we* have minds, because Descartes's method of doubt has shown that the one thing we cannot doubt is that we ourselves exist as thinking things. But how can anyone be sure that other people even *have* minds at all? After all, to be *rationally* sure of something we need to have better evidence than we have got in this case. For all that the evidence we have can show, they might be mindless automata, programmed to produce behaviour which merely simulates mindful behaviour – as a parrot produces sounds which resemble human meaningful speech, but without the intention to say anything mean-ingful. So though we may *guess* that there are other minds, and though it may be convenient for practical purposes to proceed as if they did, if we want to talk of really *knowing* something in the strict sense, maybe each of us has to say 'I might be the only conscious being, the only being with a mind, in the whole universe'. This is a version of the philosophical doctrine called 'solipsism' (from the Latin *solus ipse*, meaning 'oneself alone'). (Notice that this is not just the claim that I might be the only conscious being left in existence, which might empirically be true – for example, after some terrible disaster which wiped out all human life except mine. The solipsist is saying rather that even the *apparent* existence of other conscious beings might just be an illusion). There is a yet more radical version of solipsism, also a consequence of Cartesian dualism, which holds that *nothing at all* might exist apart from myself, since the only evidence I have for the existence of anything outside my own con-sciousness is the ideas of things which I have in my mind. For our purposes, however, we shall talk mainly about solipsism as it affects other minds, since that is most relevant to the theme of this book.

The thought that I might be alone in the universe, and that other people, including those I love most dearly, might be just robots or zombies, programmed in such a way that I am deceived into thinking that they are people just like me, is profoundly disturbing. It is also, of course, literally crazy – it is a mark of some forms of severe mental illness that the sufferer thinks in these terms. For everyday practical purposes, moreover, as said above, we need to proceed on the assumption that other people are people like ourselves, with thoughts and feelings which they can at least communicate to us, even if we may not share them, in the sense of having the same thoughts and feelings ourselves. This assumption works reasonably well most of the time, though there may be occasions when it lets us down. I myself remember an occasion when I was visiting the Edinburgh Waxworks and went to speak to what I took to be an attendant standing on the stairs, only to discover that it too was just a waxwork. But this kind of mistake simply reinforces the point: I *did* discover, to my embarrassment, that I had got it wrong, and discovered it very quickly and easily. So why can't we just set aside solipsism as another silly philosophical idea, the product of too much time spent in abstract thinking in overheated studies?

For practical purposes, of course, we can and must set it aside. But it is worth paying some attention to the doctrine in a book like this, since seeing what the arguments against it are can help us to understand how philosophers might have got into this tangle, and that in turn can reveal something more about the whole idea of 'having a mind', and about the ways in which we actually get knowledge of other minds. First of all, we need to see how the problem arises – why there is a difficulty about 'other minds' at all. One crucial thing about a mind, as we saw before, is *subjectivity*. Each person has his or her own mind: or, putting it differently, each person uses the words 'I' and 'my' (at least in direct speech) in relation to him- or herself. When I say 'I think that it is going to rain', and you say 'Yes, I think so too', we are expressing the same thought in one sense (the thought that it is going to rain), but in another way each of us is expressing a different thought (you yours and I mine). 'I', 'my' and 'mine', used in this way, are what are often called 'token-reflexive' expressions, that is, expressions which have a different reference in different contexts of use.

I can't think your thoughts (in the latter sense) and you can't think mine. That is in a way a consequence of the token-reflexivity of words like 'I' and 'mine', but it is a little misleading to say that. The token-reflexivity itself reflects the fact that my thoughts go on in me and yours in you, and that we are separate persons. We use the words as we do to mark a distinction which exists in reality. This separateness does not, of course, affect the possibility of my understanding, maybe even agreeing with, your thoughts: but understanding a thought is not the same as thinking it. The point being made here is even more obvious if we consider emotions and sensations. If someone else is in deep distress (perhaps at the death of someone they were very close to), or is suffering intense physical pain, I can sympathize with their distress or their pain. I may even express my sympathy by saying 'I feel your pain'. But I do not and cannot *literally* feel someone else's pain or distress in the way I feel my own. The most I can do is to use my imagination to induce what I take to be a similar feeling inside myself. That may well help me to feel more sympathetic, but it is not the same as feeling the other person's pain. This is just one instance of something we are all familiar with: the sense which we sometimes get of the impenetrability of another's mind – what is it *really* like to be you?

There is something tragic about this, a suggestion of the essential solitude of the individual, that we are ultimately isolated from each other. Many poets, novelists and dramatists have taken up this theme: for instance, the Russian poet Anna Akhmatova speaks in one of her poems of a barrier between people which friendship, or even passion, cannot break through. But it is an inescapable fact of life, part of what it means to have a mind. And it is this fact of the separateness of selves which gives to solipsism whatever force it has. Nevertheless, we have to set against this sense of isolation the opposing intuition we have, that human communication, however difficult, is at least sometimes possible. Even the very fact that we can talk to each other about the sense of solitude – that we can understand what Akhmatova is getting at in her poem – seems to undermine that sense.

So are there any philosophical arguments *against* solipsism? One way of approaching the topic is again derived from Wittgenstein (though other philosophers have taken a very similar line). Wittgenstein conducts a 'thought-experiment', constructing a hypothetical situation which may shed some light on the nature of the problem. Suppose, he says, that each of us carried round with us, all the time, a beetle in a box (to make the argument work, I think we have to assume that beetles didn't exist outside these boxes). Only the person who owned a particular box could look inside it and see his or her beetle. So clearly no one would have any means of knowing what the contents of anyone else's box were: for all I know, all the other boxes besides my own might be empty. This is as near as possible analogous to the solipsist position about thoughts and feelings. But there is an obvious question that one could ask about the 'beetle-in-a-box' story which could also be raised about solipsism. If there is no way in which I can compare what is in my box with what is in anyone else's, and if there is no other way in which I can be acquainted with beetles, how do I know that what I have is a 'beetle'? Knowing what a word means is knowing how to use it, to apply it correctly in a number of cases: but if I can only know of one instance of the expression, then I can't know what to call it *even in this one instance*. Similarly, the solipsist who claims to know of thoughts, feelings, sensations, etc., only from her own case can't even know that what she herself has are 'thoughts', 'feelings' and 'sensations', since she has nothing to compare them with. If I were the only conscious being in the universe, I couldn't even express my view, since I wouldn't know what 'conscious' meant.

The analogy between solipsism and the beetle-in-a-box case is not perfect. Even if I can't experience beetles except in this one case, I can still say, on the basis of my wider experience, that there is *something* in my box which may not be in anyone else's, even if I can't specify it more precisely. But thoughts, feelings and sensations are supposed by the solipsist to be a special kind of thing with which one *can* only be acquainted in one's own case: there is no way allowed therefore for one even to give meaning to the vague word 'something' in this situation. The essence of the argument is that, if there is no way, even in principle, in which I can know that other people have minds, then there is no way in which I can know that I do. The ultimate consequence of trying to be a solipsist is not the conclusion that there might be only one mind in the universe, but that there is no mind in the universe, not even mine. (Strictly, one can't even say *that*, since it presupposes that we know what a 'mind' is, and we couldn't know that from our own case alone: *what* is it that I am supposed to have which no other being has?)

There is another way of putting this anti-solipsistic argument, to be found for instance in Merleau-Ponty. The only way in which I can know what it means to be alone is to know what it means *not* to be alone. The terrible vision in Akhmatova's poem of not being able to communicate with other people only has any force for us because we know what it is to communicate with others, since we do it every day. Knowing what anything is is knowing what it can be contrasted with, so solipsism can frighten us as a possibility only because it is not actually the case.

All these arguments, however, are likely to seem a little contrived. Solipsism, as said earlier, is not the doctrine that we are as a matter of fact alone, but that the *appearance* of not being alone might be an illusion. We may, in other words, be able to refer to our own minds because we *think* we can compare them with those of other people, but that thought might be tragically mistaken. We think and act as if we were not alone in the universe: but maybe, the solipsist says, we are deceiving ourselves about this. What is terrifying about this thought is perhaps not so much the idea of being alone but the idea of living in a world of illusion – the thought that all the relationships we most cherish might be mere fantasies.

All the same, we still need to take seriously the point which Merleau-Ponty makes: that, even to make sense of being alone, we need to be able to know what it means *not* to be alone. Could we know what that means if we had not had actual experience of the existence of other people with minds? Some might argue that we could: if we can at least *imagine* what it would be like to encounter a real other mind, then we could understand what being alone in the universe is like. But what would it mean to imagine that, if we had no actual experience to base the imagining on? It seems easy enough to say, but when one tries to work out what such a supposition would actually mean, it seems to fall apart. We know what it means to be lonely only because we have actual experience of relating to other people, or at least of seeing other people relate to each other. But the solipsistic world would be one in which there would not even be the *possibility* of that. In that sense, solipsism seems to be, not just false, but actually inconceivable – ultimately, we can't even understand what the solipsist is trying to say. (And perhaps that is the reason why we regard professions of belief in solipsism as a symptom of mental disorder.)

III

If solipsism is inconceivable, we need to go back a stage and ask how anyone ever thought it was an intelligible position. It gets some plausibility, as said earlier, from the separateness of other minds and the impossibility of my having your thoughts and vice versa. But even to say that other minds are separate is to admit that they exist, and so is inconsistent with solipsism as a philosophical doctrine. Solipsism in the strict sense, as has also been said, arises when one thinks in Cartesian fashion of a 'mind' as a separate substance from a 'body'. So that is where we should look if we want to pull up this strange plant of solipsism by its roots. The most relevant feature of dualism is that it separates what is mental from its bodily expressions. For the dualist, it is one thing to have a thought and quite another to express that thought in words; one thing to feel amused, another to smile; one thing to be in pain, another to cry out; and so on. And of course, these things *are* separable: we can have thoughts, feelings and sensations which we don't express in any way detectable by others. A solitary person has many thoughts which are never in fact put into words; a dour person may be amused without smiling; a stoic may refuse to reveal her pain to others. Conversely, an empty headed person may make statements without thought; an actor may smile without being amused; and an attention seeker may utter cries of pain without feeling the relevant sensations. But is there another sense in which no gap is possible between what goes on in our minds and our outward expressions – one which would undermine solipsism?

Wittgenstein's thought-experiment of the beetle in the box has already been referred to, and some criticisms of it have been made. But it may nevertheless suggest a way in which one could say that there is an inescapable link between the mental and its bodily expression. (Merleau-Ponty's conception of subjectivity as essentially embodied points in the same direction, and some of the discussion of that conception in Chapter 3 is relevant here.) Let us take the relatively simple case of feeling pain first. Pain is certainly something that one feels 'inside' one: it is a sensation. Other people can't literally *see* my pain, in the way they can see the wound which may be causing it. Even if the neurologist's instruments may reveal that appropriate nerves are firing, she is still not seeing my pain (indeed in some cases my nerves may be firing in this way when I am not feeling any pain, e.g. because I am so distracted by other sensations, or have a high pain-threshold). Equally, if I am in pain, I necessarily *know* I am, without any need for observing my behaviour: just to feel pain is to know one is in pain. I may be mistaken about the *cause* of my pain –

thinking for instance that it has some organic cause when it doesn't. But that I am in pain is, it seems, something I can't be mistaken about.

All the same (and this is where Wittgenstein comes in), we have to ask how I know what 'being in pain' is. Did I learn that by having this internal sensation and identifying it as a 'pain'? But 'pain' is a word in a shared language: could I know that what I feel was pain unless I knew it was also what other people were talking about when they said, for example, 'I've got this terrible pain in my wrist'? And how could I know this if pain were *just* an internal sensation to which no one except the person in pain had access? To know that I am in pain, I must know that 'pain' is the word for this particular kind of sensation which I feel when, for instance, I cut my finger. To know that is to be able to use the word correctly: someone who told her doctor she had a pain in her head when in fact she was feeling unusually euphoric (say) would be saying something false, just as much as someone who said she was seeing a rose when in fact she was seeing a dandelion. If there isn't any point to talking of 'correct' and 'incorrect' use of an expression like 'pain', then the expression has no real meaning – it can mean whatever the speaker chooses to mean by it, and that is the same as meaning nothing. (The argument against a purely private language again.)

In the case of the rose and the dandelion, it is possible to bring in others to correct mistaken usage. Someone who knows more about flowers than the speaker can say 'No, that's not a rose, that's a dandelion': if the speaker takes this correction to heart, she is not likely to make the same mistake in future. But how can this correction be possible in the case of 'pain'? Only because the word is not used only to refer to some private inner sensation, but is used in a certain publicly observable context. Pain is what we typically feel when we are injured in some way, and when we have a spontaneous tendency to cry out and to behave in other characteristic ways (facial expressions, clutching the affected part of the body, twisting and writhing, and so on): in early childhood, when most of us first learn to talk about pain, this will be a tendency which is always, or almost always, manifested in actual behaviour. Pain is also something which naturally elicits sympathy from other human beings, or at least from those who are close to us. So a child may well learn the concept of pain by instinctively crying out when she has the relevant sensation and receiving a sympathetic response from a parent, which may well be expressed in part by using the word 'pain' or some equivalent. Later, she may add the words 'I've got a pain' to the cry, or even substitute the former for the latter. If the surrounding circumstances and consequences don't seem appropriate, the child's use of the word may be corrected. If, for example, the child is grinning broadly and playing in an untroubled fashion when she says that she has a pain, and especially if there are none of the usual consequences of being in pain, an adult may say 'You're not really in pain at all: I think you're just pretending, you're really perfectly happy'.

Once the child has got the concept of pain in this way, she is in a position to use it in a way which separates the outward expression from the sensation. She can both engage in pretence and play-acting – crying out when she does not have the sensation; and have the sensation but learn not to express it. Neither of these possibilities implies in any way that there is not a natural connection between pain and its outward expressions. We can be taken in by play-acting only because crying out is typically an expression of pain; and we are annoyed when the play-acting is deliberately engaged in in order to arouse our sympathies, because the person is using the natural association with certain forms of expression in order to deceive us. And on the other hand stoicism is seen as something admirable because the stoic is exercising self-control, inhibiting the natural expressions of pain, presumably for some respectable motive, like sparing others the need to feel sympathy.

The upshot is that we cannot ultimately separate the feeling of pain from at least the possibility of expressing it in some publicly accessible form, either by means of natural expressions like crying out and writhing, or by means of verbal language, most notably the use of the word 'pain'. Of course, no one could be said to feel pain if they had no sensations of the relevant kind; but equally no one could be said to feel pain unless they could express it in some appropriate and publicly intelligible way: at most, they could be said to have some kind of indeterminate sensation which was neither one of pain nor of euphoria nor of any other specifiable kind. In this sense, being in pain is an essentially communicable experience, social as well as individual.

This becomes more obvious still when we turn to more complex mental states like having a thought or a feeling. Here intentionality enters in. One cannot, as was argued in an earlier chapter, have a thought or a feeling which is not *about* something. In order to specify what thoughts or feelings someone is having, it is not enough to specify what is going on 'inside' them (whether metaphorically in their Cartesian soul or literally in their materialist brain): one must also specify the relation in which they stand to something or someone outside them. Someone's thought might, for instance, be about Descartes, and that would be a different thought from one about Aristotle, even if (which is possible) the brain-processes involved in the two thoughts were identical – the same neurons were firing in the same way. Furthermore, one can specify that they are different thoughts without knowing anything about brain-processes. Similarly, feeling angry about the school bully is a different feeling from feeling angry about your best friend who has let you down, even though, probably, the biochemistry of anger is the same in both cases. And again, one can distinguish the one feeling from the other without knowing anything about biochemistry.

In the case of feelings, there is a further element. A feeling of anger differs, obviously, from a feeling of fear: here the biochemistry of the two feelings is certainly different, but we can distinguish the one feeling from the other again without any knowledge of biochemistry. In this case, we do so, not so much by differentiating their objects (we may, after all, feel anger at and fear of the same thing or person – the school bully, for example), but by the relation in which we stand to the object of our emotions. To feel anger at the school bully is to feel aggressive towards him, to want to do him harm; to feel afraid of him is to want to take avoiding action, to keep out of his way if we can. Thus, different feelings have different natural expressions in our behaviour. The two feelings are therefore distinguished, not just by what goes on inside us, but also by the difference in our relation to someone or something outside us, typically (though not always) expressed in behaviour.

In ways like this, what it is to have a particular thought or feeling cannot be defined simply in terms of what goes on inside us but must also involve our relationship to objects outside us, expressed in ways of behaving towards them. Putting it another way, we learn what it means to feel afraid, for example, when we learn how people who are afraid react to what they are afraid of. And, even more obviously, we learn what it is to have a thought when we acquire the language which enables us both to understand others' thoughts and to express our own. If all this is correct, then Descartes cannot be right to think of thoughts, feelings and sensations as things which simply go on inside us and are quite separate from any observable expressions. Thoughts, feelings and sensations do indeed go on inside us: but that inside cannot be separated from its possible outward expression. If so, then as a *philosophical* position, solipsism cannot even get started. We can only say that we ourselves have minds, i.e. have thoughts, feelings and sensations, because we can use the relevant concepts, and we have to learn those concepts from our interactions with the minds of others. In that way, mine *couldn't* be the only possible mind in the universe. In a particular case, as in the example of the wax-work given earlier, someone may be mistaken, or unsure, about whether what looks like another person is indeed one. But that mistake can be remedied as long as we know what 'having a mind' means: as in this case, if I asked the waxwork a question and got no reply or prodded it and got no response, I would quickly discover whether or not it had a mind. In other cases, it might be a more difficult and protracted process, but in principle it could always be decided one way or the other.

IV

Even if philosophical solipsism is ruled out, however, there remains a more practical problem of other minds. We all know, as was said earlier, that it is possible to keep our thoughts and feelings, and even our sensations, to ourselves, and most of us do so sometimes – either out of politeness, or reserve or sometimes in a deliberate attempt to deceive other people. The fact that we cannot separate thoughts, etc., from the *possibility* of expressing them does not imply that they cannot be separated from *actual* expression on particular occasions. It is part of the nature of what we mean by our mental life that it does go on 'inside' us in this sense: what we have on any particular occasion is still a thought even if it is not expressed, even if it could not be a thought if it could not in principle be expressed. Of course, we can only learn to control the expression of our thoughts once we are able to express them: but nevertheless this is something which we can learn to do.

This is what creates the practical problem about other minds. We encounter others who smile, or frown, or say things, or behave in a loving way, and we know that it is possible to do any of these things without really meaning them. How can we know that this is not one of the occasions when they are pretending to feel or think what they seem to be feeling or thinking? How can we *ever* know in any particular case what someone else is thinking or feeling? (There is also the situation in which the other person appears not to be reacting at all, and we wonder whether this shows that she does not have any feelings or views, or whether she has feelings which she is simply not exhibiting, and if so what those feelings are.) This is different from philosophical solipsism, since to wonder what someone's real feelings are implies that they *have* real feelings. But it could be called a form of solipsism, since it says that on any given occasion we cannot know what someone else is thinking or feeling, so that any of our *specific* judgements about people's thoughts and feelings could as a matter of fact be mistaken.

This seems less crazy a view than philosophical scepticism, since it rests on the real experiences we sometimes have of our own or other people's insincerity, or of talking at cross purposes, or just feeling bewildered about what another person's real attitudes and feelings might be. Personal experience is here reinforced by the testimony of novelists, poets and playwrights about the difficulties of human communication. In order to see what kind of reply could be made to this less crazy form of solipsism, we need first to ask what it *means* to 'know what someone else is thinking or feeling'. Given what has been said earlier, it is not like knowing what is going on in a locked and windowless room, since thoughts and feelings have been argued to be more than inner processes. Rather, what it seems to mean is being able to understand the reasons for someone's acting as they do. Someone says to us, 'I do so admire your work'. We wonder whether they really mean it, or are simply saying so in order to be flattering and so get something from us. In other words, we think we cannot decide between two possible interpretations or explanations of what they say. If it was impossible in principle to decide with any degree of certainty, then we should say that we could not know what they really felt. On the other hand, if there was some way in which we could decide one way or the other, we could reasonably say that we could know, however uncertain we might feel at the moment.

This might suggest to some that we are making use of the 'theory of mind' referred to earlier. Then it would be parallel to a situation in science, in which two or more alternative explanations of some phenomenon were possible. We should need to collect evidence for and against each explanation: if explanation A were correct, then we should expect such-and-such to happen, whereas if explanation

B were correct we should expect something different. Equally, in either case we should expect certain things *not* to happen if that explanation were correct. And then we could try to resolve the issue by looking to see whether these expected consequences did or did not happen. For instance, when what we now call AIDS was discovered, it was thought by some to be explained by the use by homosexuals of certain kinds of sexual stimulants. If this were the correct explanation, then we should expect that AIDS symptoms were more likely to appear when people used these stimulants, and should definitely not appear when those who had them had not engaged in sex using such stimulants. These consequences did not follow, so the proffered explanation was clearly mistaken. The explanation which almost everyone now accepts is that the symptoms of AIDS are caused by a virus, the human immunodeficiency virus, which is transmitted from one sufferer to another by means of bodily fluids. This explanation is confirmed by the fact that only those who have received bodily fluids from someone with AIDS, through sex, or blood transfusions, or sharing hypodermic needles, or in some other way, have the disease; by the fact that the virus is found in those with the disease, and so on. This kind of evidence does not amount to a *proof* of the explanation's correctness, but it does give us enough support to believe that we now know what causes AIDS.

So is it like this with knowing someone else's thoughts and feelings? Well, what actually happens? Very often, especially in relatively simple cases, we have no doubt at all what is going on in someone's mind. Someone, clearly accidentally, appears to cut his finger on a knife and screams out: we have no doubt that he is not play-acting, but is genuinely in pain. We may come to think differently if a moment later he stops screaming, laughs loudly and says 'I fooled you'. Again, if he stops screaming and we see a camera running nearby and pointing in his direction, a person running up with a fresh supply of tomato ketchup, and the scene being repeated after a man with a clapper-board says 'Take Two'. But if none of these things happen, and the man goes on screaming and we rush over to offer first aid and he finds it comforting to have his wound bandaged, then we should become more and more certain that the pain is real. There is always the possibility, of course, that our certainty is still misplaced, but the longer the man goes on behaving like someone in pain, the more reasonable it becomes to say we 'know' the pain is real and not feigned. It would indeed be inhuman to harbour suspicions unless we had some very good reason for doing so – if the man was an actor on a stage and we were in the theatre audience, for instance, or if we knew the man to be an incorrigible practical joker, or if we saw that the 'knife' was in fact a cardboard replica.

Is this like formulating a scientific hypothesis to explain the phenomenon and then testing it against the evidence? It has some similarities, clearly, but there are also significant differences. The story just told seems more one about a natural or spontaneous way to interpret certain kinds of behaviour (he's hurt himself and is in pain), which may later be altered or modified in the light of evidence, but need not be. If nothing had come along to make us suspicious, we should not say that our initial reaction was just a hypothesis which had so far not been falsified: we should simply go on accepting it and, if asked, should say that we *knew* he was in pain. Even if we do become suspicious of our original interpretation, we might wonder whether that is like coming to reject a hypothesis on the basis of contrary evidence. It is not so much that we notice that the facts contradict our original hypothesis, as in the AIDS case, because they don't: actors on a stage or a film set, who may be pretending to cut themselves, may still feel real pain and cry out for some other reason, as may practical jokers using cardboard replica knives. Rather, part of the concept of pain that we have learned is that pain typically happens when people hurt themselves and that the typical expressions of pain include such things as screams, bodily contortions, exclamations such as 'Ouch', clutching the affected part and so on. But someone with a sophisticated grasp of the concept of pain will realize that in any particular case people can feel it without physically harming themselves, and can either not express it at all or express it in a range of other ways apart from those just mentioned. That is, we do not have here a hypothesis to be tested against the facts so much as a way of interpreting certain kinds of human behaviour, which may be modified in the light of our judgement of the significance of the surrounding facts.

When we move on to more complex kinds of human thought and feeling, the difference from testing a scientific hypothesis seems to become more obvious. Suppose I fail to turn up for an appointment with my friend. He had said to me earlier how much he wanted to see me this time, since he wanted to discuss something which was very important to him and on which he needed my advice. And I simply forget to turn up, because I was so much absorbed by the football match on television. Next day, I bump into him on the street and say how sorry I am to have let him down in this way. He replies that it's all right, not to worry. In my guilt, however, I wonder what he *really* feels – is he really ready to forgive and forget, or is he just too afraid to show his anger? Is there something about the tone in which he says 'It's all right' which indicates that it really *isn't* all right as far as he is concerned? I just don't know, but I *want* to know. How could I go about trying to decide? I could wait a while, and see how he goes on. If our friendship continues, and is as warm as ever, then perhaps I might come to believe that his forgiving words were genuinely meant as such. On the other hand, if things were never the same again between us, then I might feel that perhaps he was genuinely angry with me, despite the surface meaning of his words. But either of these interpretations might still be mistaken. He might have felt angry, but be such a strong character that he overcame his anger for the sake of our friendship. Or perhaps he might genuinely have not been all that bothered by my thoughtlessness, but we might have drifted apart for some other reason. How seriously we take any of these indications, and how confident we feel in saying that we *know* how someone feels will depend on a judgement we have to make.

The difference from the scientific case then is that the evidence for and against a particular interpretation is not a specifiable set of consequences whose presence or absence tends to verify or falsify the hypothesis we form: rather, it is a somewhat indeterminate range of indications in the context and in the mode of expression whose relevance we have to judge. It is more like telling a story and deciding how it should go on if it is to be plausible. This means that not only can we not prove that a particular interpretation is correct or incorrect, but there may be, at least in the more complex cases, no way of deciding between different and rival interpretations. Even the person him- or herself may, in such complex cases, be unable to decide definitely what he or she was feeling or thinking. This is not a problem, then, only about 'other' minds, it is a problem about mind.

We learn the factors which tell for or against a particular interpretation, whether of our own or of someone else's behaviour, in the course of learning what is meant by words like 'thought', 'feeling', 'sensation' and so on. We learn the meaning of these words, as said earlier, from our interactions with others in society, and their meanings are not precisely defined, but embodied in a vague and rather loose set of criteria, whose application is a matter of judgement and imagination. This is a further difference from scientific or theoretical explanation. If I explain why my pen falls to the floor by invoking the earth's gravitational attraction, I give a simple theoretical explanation, using the precisely defined concept of gravity. This is a concept which gets its meaning from its role in a theory devised to make sense of various kinds of observations – the fall of objects to the earth, the orbits of planets, the rise and fall of tides and so on – and the very precision of its formulation leaves no room for doubt about when it is correctly applied and when it is not. But the concepts which we use in what eliminativists would call our 'folk psychology' are developed, not as part of a theory to bring together different observations, but as part of our social life together, part of our sharing of thoughts and feelings with each other. They cannot be precisely defined, so that there is ample room for doubt in many cases about whether they are correctly applied. It is here that we should look for the roots of the practical problem of solipsism: it is not so much that our thoughts and feelings are incommunicable, as that there is always room in any given case for doubt about whether what seems to be communicated is really what is thought or felt.

There are further complications, arising from the fact that it is possible for a person to conceal their thoughts and feelings – to choose to put out of play the natural expressions of what they are thinking and feeling. The criteria do not uniquely determine the correct application of the concept anyway: things get even worse when no criteria seem to be available. Connected with this, perhaps, is the idea which is sometimes expressed that our deepest thoughts and feelings are somehow inexpressible in words. Quite what this idea amounts to is not at all clear. Someone may, for instance, say to his beloved 'I love you', and then feel that this conventional sentence is too weak to really express how he feels about her. It does not capture the full intensity of his devotion, so that in this way the most important part of his feelings is unexpressed. But it obviously does not follow from that that his emotions are *inexpressible*. The very fact that he can say how the conventional form of words falls short in itself implies that he *can* express his deepest feelings: if he could not, how could he say how the words fall short? We do use lots of clichés and formulaic sentences in our conversation with each other, and in this sense our expression of our thoughts and feelings (especially our feelings) may be inadequate. But much can be conveyed by other, non-linguistic, means – by our tone of voice, our body-language, the look in our eyes or our gestures – which makes up for the deficiencies of our verbal expression, and we can improve our verbal expression itself by using less conventional forms such as poetry. That our tendency to hide our feelings, or to use inadequate language in expressing them, may often make it hard for others really to penetrate our minds is undeniable: but it does not follow that the mind of another person is somehow intrinsically impenetrable because of the privacy and incommunicability of their thoughts and feelings.

It was said earlier that thinking about solipsism, crazy though that doctrine may be, could be useful in clarifying our thoughts about mind. So what have we learned about the more general question from this discussion? First, that our mental life is not to be equated with some *purely* 'inner' world: our minds are part of the public, social world. What I think and feel is what I can communicate to others, and in that sense exists in the space between us as much as inside me. Knowing the minds of others is difficult, but no more so than knowing one's own mind. If I can't find the words to express my feelings to someone else adequately, so that they do not know how I really feel, then by the same token I cannot find words to describe my own feelings to myself, so that I do not really know what my own feelings are. And if I cannot put my thoughts into words which will convey them to others, then the thoughts themselves must be inadequately formed, not known properly even to me. (Think of the way we sometimes find out what we think only by trying to put our thoughts into words and so finding the right words to express them.)

It is nevertheless an important feature of the mental that it does go on 'inside' us. Thoughts and feelings, as we have seen, though they must be expressible, do not need to be actually expressed: it is part of the nature of mental processes and states that they can be kept to ourselves, and we have also all sorts of motives, respectable and not so respectable, for so keeping them. It is a mark of social sophistication to be able to think without moving our lips; and it is one of the symptoms of certain kinds of mental disorder that some of our private thoughts are uttered out loud. This ability to keep our thoughts and feelings to ourselves is what gives sense to the idea of the mental life as the inner life. It is an essential part of what was called in an earlier chapter the 'subjectivity' of mental life: I have my thoughts and you have yours; I cannot have your thoughts, even if I may have thoughts which agree with yours. This is not incompatible with the essential communicability of thoughts and feelings – quite the contrary, we can only speak of communication when the person communicating is separate from the person receiving the communication. I do not communicate my own thoughts to myself, I just have them; I communicate them to someone else, who has his or her own thoughts. But there certainly is an appearance of paradox here: if I am genuinely a separate subject from you, so that you and I cannot have the same thoughts and feelings, how is it possible for me to communicate my thoughts and feelings to you? But on the other hand, *unless* you and I are separate subjects, talk of communication would be meaningless. Whether or not this apparent paradox can be resolved, both the separateness of minds and the possibility of communication between them seem to be essential features of what we mean by 'mind'.

CHAPTER 6

REASONS AND CAUSES

I

So where have we got to in thinking about what it is to have a mind? In Chapters 1 and 2, we examined arguments for and against two traditional philosophical approaches to this question – Cartesian dualism and what we called 'classical materialism'. Despite their opposition, they were seen to share one common feature: both saw the question as concerned with what kind of thing a 'mind' was, what kind of 'stuff' it was made of. For the dualist, a mind is a special kind of thing, different from any other kind of thing in the known universe, because it is made of a unique kind of stuff – occupying no space, having no dimensions and no position relative to other things. (So strictly speaking, it can't be described as being literally 'inside' the body it is supposed to 'inhabit'.) For the classical materialist, on the other hand, what was traditionally called a 'mind' would better be described as a 'brain', which is made of the same kind of stuff as everything else – what is referred to as 'matter', in the sense of what is studied by physical science and governed ultimately by the laws of physics. Different kinds of materialists are distinguished largely by whether they want to 'reduce' psychology (using the concepts of 'thought', 'desire', 'wish', etc.) to the more obviously physical science of neurophysiology (using such concepts as 'neuron firings'), or simply to eventually replace an independent psychology by a 'completed neuroscience'. We also saw that there is a third, rather ill-defined, group, called 'functionalists', who were officially neither dualists nor materialists, but who compared minds to computer programs, 'software' rather than 'hardware'. The software can be realized in any kind of stuff, so it is rather more abstract in character than the brain, or even the soul. Nevertheless, we argued that the functionalist approach does not differ sufficiently from traditional materialism to avoid its difficulties.

Starting in Chapter 3, we looked at a different kind of approach to the whole question, which was developed further by the discussions of Chapters 4 and 5. Instead of starting from the assumption that 'mind' must be the name of a kind of thing, made of a certain kind of stuff, it was suggested that we should start by looking at how we think and talk about our mental lives in everyday life, before we even begin to try to construct philosophical or scientific theories about minds. If we do this, it was argued, we shall see that when we talk about our mental lives, we are talking about certain kinds of things that people do (and maybe, in some cases, that members of other species do). They have thoughts about the world, some more reasonable than others. They feel emotions about people, things, situations and places, of different degrees of intensity and appropriateness to their objects. They want certain things. They remember certain things and forget others. They have intentions to act in certain ways, and sometimes act on them. They feel pain and pleasure. And so on. Talk about these mental states and processes implies nothing about what kind or kinds of stuff human beings are made of, or what is responsible for our thinking, feeling, wishing, intending and the rest. And the very fact that our mental lives are so varied, and that it is hard sometimes to decide whether or to what extent the 'mind' is involved in what we do, suggests strongly that 'mind' is not the name of some distinct part of ourselves, but a general term for referring to a loosely defined sort of human activities.

Ryle expresses this approach by saying that we should not see human beings either as 'ghosts in machines' as dualists do, nor as 'machines without ghosts', as materialists do, but simply as human beings. Merleau-Ponty, similarly, focuses primarily on the human being, as an embodied subjectivity, rather than on 'minds' or 'bodies' on their own. Another modern philosopher, Peter Strawson (Strawson 1959: ch. 3) puts a very similar point by arguing that the primary concept ought not to be that of a mind or a body, but that of a 'person', a being who has both psychological or mental properties, like having certain thoughts, and physical or bodily properties, like being blue-eyed. We can ask about someone's opinions about stem-cell research, or about their waist measurement, and these are clearly questions about the same person.

This puts the whole question of what it is to have a mind in a different light. We start now from the human being, or person, so that to say what it is to have a mind is to say what it is about persons that leads us to describe them as having a mental life, or 'psychological properties'; and the problem of the 'mind–body relationship' is no longer that of the interaction between two things, but of the way in which the psychological properties of people relate to their physical properties, and of how both are involved in the life of the person as a whole. It could be expressed like this: 'people have both minds and bodies' means 'people are psychological beings as well as biological beings'. Then the question becomes what is meant by these two types of being. That involves asking, first, what are the characteristics of psychological properties and how do they compare with those of biological or physical properties? And then asking what the answer to that question tells us about what it means to be a psychological as well as a biological being.

We may not be able to draw a hard-and-fast line round the human activities which involve the mind, but we do seem to recognize, as suggested in Chapter 3, that what is at the heart of our idea of the mental tends to have some characteristic features. In order to draw the various threads of this book together in this final chapter, it would be helpful to review and expand on the discussion of these features. First of all, it is 'intentional'. Thinking, as we have said, is necessarily thinking *about* something, emotions are felt *about* someone or something, wishes or desires are *for* something and so on. The something or someone to which our thoughts, feelings, desires or whatever are directed need not actually exist: plots against my life, for instance, do not need to really exist in order to be what I am afraid of. But I could not have a thought, feeling, wish, etc., which was not directed towards some such 'intentional object'. The intentional object therefore cannot be the *cause* of my thought or feeling or desire: a non-existent thing cannot be the cause of anything. And something is an intentional object *under some description or other*. If I am thinking about Tony Blair, I am not necessarily thinking about the present Prime Minister of the UK or about the present Leader of the Labour Party. I might not know that Mr Blair held these positions, but could still think about the man just as the individual he is. I might therefore know, say, what height Mr Blair was, but not realize that this was also the height of the Prime Minister. What defines my thought, feeling, desire, etc., as the one it is, is not some internal feature of the 'mental process or state' itself, but its relation to its specific intentional object considered under the relevant description. Some philosophers have said (and the importance of this will become clearer shortly) that psychological activities, as intentional, have a 'meaning' for the person in question. The meaning for me is the description of the intentional object which I could recognize as what I was thinking or feeling about, wishing for, desiring, etc.: for instance, 'Mr Blair as current UK Prime Minister'.

As we have also seen, however, not everything that we call 'mental' or 'psychological' seems to be intentional. Sensations of (physical) pain, for example, do not seem to have intentional objects: what differentiates pains is not the object they are directed towards (if any), but their internal qualities of intensity and type and location, and sometimes what causes them. I may have two pains, one intense, the other mild; one acute, the other chronic; one more of a dull ache, the other more throbbing; one in my arm and one in my toe; one caused by the pin sticking in me, the other caused by banging into the door when I tripped. Pains, however, though often cited by philosophers talking about the mind, seem to be peripheral to our idea of the mental.

The other characteristic of the mental does seem, as we saw, to be shared both by such peripheral states as pain and by the core examples such as thinking and feeling. This is what we called earlier 'subjectivity'. Again, we can repeat and add to the previous discussion. A thought, or a desire, or an emotion, or a pain can exist only by being *someone's*: there must be a subject to have them. The idea of a thought hanging about in the atmosphere without a subject does not seem to make sense. And each subject's thoughts, etc., must be distinct existences from each other subject's. You and I can, of course, in one sense have the same thought: we may both be thinking, for instance, 'Dualism is a confused theory of mind'. But, although the content of our thoughts may be the same in this way, there is a clear sense in which there are *two* thoughts here – yours and mine. My thought belongs with other thoughts of mine; yours belongs with your other thoughts. I can't have your thought (in this sense) and you can't have mine.

The biological properties and operations of human beings do not seem to be either intentional or subjective in the senses just explained. The beat of the heart, or the workings of the digestive system or lungs, are not defined as what they are by the intentional object they are directed towards, under a certain description which someone could recognize: they have no 'meaning' in that sense. They are what they are, no matter what anyone thinks about them, or even if no one thinks about them at all. A heart-beat, for example, is part, as Descartes saw, of the 'machinery' of the body: defined as what it is by its internal properties, and perhaps also by its role in relation to other parts of the machinery (just like the cogs in a piece of clockwork, or the pistons in a steam engine). Like any piece of machinery, its processes are governed by ordinary laws of physics and chemistry, and behave as they do in accordance with those laws. And one person's heart is much the same as another's, in the sense at least that its workings are governed by the same physico-chemical laws as any other heart. This is shown by the fact that we can transplant one person's heart, or even an animal heart, into another person's body, and, if the transplant 'takes', then it will perform the same operations as the original one. A heart can even be kept beating artificially when it is not attached to any body. In that sense, a biological organ does not *essentially* belong to a 'subject', in the way that a thought, or a feeling, or a wish or desire do. Even a human brain, at least if we leave out of account its connection with mental life, can be viewed as a biological mechanism: it performs its functions in broadly similar ways no matter whose brain it is, governed by the same laws of physics, and a particular set of neurons can be identified as what it is by its internal properties, without reference to any 'meaning' or intentional object.

II

So, considered as purely biological beings, people do not have subjectivity or intentionality: they are simply 'organisms' of a particular species, which function in broadly similar ways to all other organisms of that species, and their functioning has no 'meaning'. They simply proceed in accordance with physical law. As psychological beings, however, people relate to the world as different subjects, each with his or her individual point of view, and their relations to their worlds have meaning for them. Putting matters in this way is likely to raise a further question. Is this distinction between a person as a biological being and a person as a psychological being just another version of Cartesian dualism? One way to deal with *this* question is to connect the biological/psychological distinction with a difference which some philosophers have seen between two ways of explaining what human beings do.

There is a tradition of thought which distinguishes between 'causal explanation' and 'reason-explanation': this tradition began in the nineteenth century in Germany, but it has many followers still, including some in the English-speaking world. Some philosophers in this tradition keep the term 'explanation' for the causal kind, and call reason-explanation 'understanding'. (Since many of the nineteenth- and early twentieth-century originators of this tradition, such as Wilhelm Dilthey, Heinrich Rickert and Max Weber, were German, they used the German words *Erklärung* (explanation) and *Verstehen* (understanding), and these German terms, especially the latter, are often found even in the non-German-speaking literature.) Causal explanation is, roughly speaking, giving an answer to the question, 'What brought this about?' or 'How did this come to be as it is?' Reason-explanation is what is given in answer to the question, 'Why is this so?' or 'What is the point or purpose of this?' There is some room for confusion here, since both the words 'cause' and 'reason' are used fairly loosely, and to some extent interchangeably, in ordinary speech, and explanation of either kind is sometimes said to be an answer to a 'Why?' question. We may ask, for example, why leaves fall from certain trees in autumn, and the appropriate answer will be in terms of the processes which bring it about that leaves fall. But even in ordinary speech, there is some suggestion of a difference between causes and reasons: if we ask what the reason for having a pedestrian crossing at a particular place is, for instance, we would want to be told what the *point* of having one there was (to protect pedestrians in a dangerous traffic area), not to be given a story of what brought it about that it was installed there (for instance, council workmen brought the equipment there and dug up the road to install it).

Aristotle makes a similar distinction in terms of two types of 'cause'. What we have called 'causes' are equivalent to what the English translations of Aristotle refer to as 'efficient causes'; while what we have called 'reasons' are equivalent to what they refer to as 'final causes'. In Aristotle, however, anything in nature has a 'final' as well as an 'efficient' cause – a reason why it exists, as well as a cause which brings it about. For example, we might be able to explain why (for what reason) an oak tree sheds its leaves in the autumn – what purpose this serves in the grand scheme of things – as well as what processes bring about the fall of leaves. In modern science, however, the idea of 'final causes' in nature has been abandoned. To talk about something as having a reason for being so seems to involve some reference to a conscious being who has had some purpose in making it so. In regard to natural processes and events, that being could only be a supernatural creator: but even scientists who believe in the existence of such a creator think it necessary to keep their religious beliefs separate from their science. From a purely scientific point of view, we have to regard nature as simply a set of processes which bring about other processes, with no purpose or point: this is just how things happen, and the question 'Why do they happen like this?' is held to have no place in a rational science.

But when we turn to human actions (or even some of the actions of non-human animals), this doesn't look so obviously wrong. For human beings do seem to act purposively, with a view to achieving some goal: this is connected in an obvious way with their intentionality and subjectivity. We can go back to the example already given. It seems at least as sensible to ask 'Why (for what reason) has a pedestrian crossing been established at this place in the road?' as to ask 'How did it come about that the crossing was established here?' The processes involved, both mechanical and administrative, in setting up a pedestrian crossing are presumably much the same wherever one is established: what interests us are the reasons the authorities had for choosing *this* place to set one up rather than some other possible site. And only an answer in terms of reasons, not one in terms of causes, will satisfy this interest.

So the philosophers in question restricted 'reason-explanation' and 'understanding' to *human actions*. Not everything which human beings do counts as an 'action' for these purposes, only those things which involve thought, feeling, etc., and to the extent that they do. Some 'things that we do' are mere movements of our body, with no involvement of mind – pure reflexes like the knee-jerk, for instance, which just happen to us and are not done for any reason. And even our actions, since we are embodied creatures, necessarily involve some movements of the body: even thinking requires brain-processes, and going for a walk involves not merely the thought of doing so or the desire which motivates it, but movements within the brain and nervous system, and of the leg muscles. But those movements which involve mind necessarily involve intentionality and subjectivity: we act with a view to achieving some object or goal which we have.

In the case of the more sophisticated, typically human, actions, as we saw in an earlier chapter, to say that they are intentional implies that the person doing the action can identify the action in terms of some concept which he or she understands. For instance, going for a walk is a sophisticated action in that sense: other animals can walk, but only human beings can literally do what we call 'going for a walk'. This is because to go for a walk involves having the ability to describe what one is doing in that way, to have the 'concept' of 'going for a walk', which one has learned by participating in a society in which that concept is used. Having that concept in turn requires one to recognize a range of possible reasons for going for a walk: to get some exercise, to take a break from one's work indoors, to enjoy the countryside and so on. Subjectivity comes in because one or more of these possible reasons must be *one's actual* reason for acting in this way on this occasion. So we can understand why someone went for a walk on a particular occasion when we are told his or her reason for doing so. This can be said to be the 'meaning' of the action (see above) for the person performing it, the 'agent'.

Mere 'movements', which don't involve the mind, can't be understood in terms of their meaning in this sense, because, as movements, they don't have one. If the doctor taps my knee, and my knee jerks, this is not the same as my jerking my knee deliberately. I don't have a *reason* for doing it, so it is pointless to ask me why I did it. In an important sense, a pure reflex is not something I *do* at all, but something which happens to me. The only way we can explain it is by giving its causes, that is, by saying what brought it about – the doctor's tap, together with certain facts about the human nervous system. Our 'meaningful' actions, as said already, also necessarily involve movements, even if it is only processes within the brain. That implies that we can explain them in two different ways, depending on the nature of our interest in them. If I am engaged in a conversation with you, then you will probably be primarily interested in the reasons why I say the things I do. But a physiologist observing our conversation from a scientific point of view might be more interested in what caused me to produce the relevant sounds – the movements of my vocal cords, etc., and perhaps also the processes in the brain which resulted in them. But notice that the way what is to be explained is described is different in the two cases, even though in a sense these are two different descriptions of the same thing. You (and I) describe what is to be explained as 'my statements' – the propositions I put forward, such as 'I trust Mr Smith'; the physiologist describes what is to be explained as 'the sounds I utter'. In this case, I am making my statement by uttering these sounds: but the two things can be distinguished. I can express my feelings about Mr Smith in writing, or by sign-language, or silently to myself without sounds or by using words in another language which have different sounds. Equally, it might be that in some other language these same sounds express a totally different proposition. We can't make statements without performing some bodily movements, but a statement can't be identified with the movements involved in making it on any particular occasion.

Movements of the body, like any other physical movements, are explained by giving their causes. The philosophers who make the 'reason/cause' distinction generally follow David Hume (1711–76) in their analysis of what is involved in stating the cause of something. For our present purposes, we do not need to go into the details or the difficulties of Hume's analysis: we can simply say that, for him, a 'cause' of some event (something which happens) is a separate event, which comes before the event to be explained (the 'effect'), and is of a type which is regularly connected with events of the effect-type. Thus, to say, for example, that a stone thrown by someone caused the window to break roughly means, on this analysis, that the impact of the stone came immediately before the breaking of the window, and that the impact of heavy objects like stones is regularly connected with the breaking of fragile things like glass. A more modern version of Hume's analysis, which connects causal explanation more closely with science, is the so-called 'covering-law model', which says (briefly) that to give a causal explanation of some event is to show that the connection between the alleged cause and the effect is an instance of a generalization, or law, which connects events of these two types. This *explains* the effect by showing how it was predictable in the circumstances.

We can now specify some of the relevant differences, according to these philosophers, between 'reason-explanation' (understanding the meaning of an action) and 'causal explanation' (showing how a movement was brought about). We causally explain the utterance of certain sounds by showing it to be an instance of a regular pattern, in which certain kinds of movements of vocal cords produce certain kinds of sounds. And we causally explain the movements of the vocal cords by showing that there is a regular connection between certain kinds of brain and nervous processes and these movements. The regular connections invoked are *general* – they have no particular reference to me or to this occasion. And they make no reference either to what these sounds *mean*: as far as this kind of explanation goes, they are just sound waves in the air, which might equally well be produced by anyone in any situation. But, if you explain my statements in terms of my reasons for making them, then you are clearly referring to *my* reasons on *this* occasion. I say that I trust Mr Smith: what you want to know is why *I* say that, and what reason I have for saying it just now.

The generalizations we appeal to in offering causal explanations of movements can be established or refuted by empirical evidence in the usual way. If asked how we know that certain movements of vocal cords produce certain sounds, we can say that they have been regularly observed to do so (or, if we want to be followers of Karl Popper, we can at least say that this generalization has at least not been falsified by empirical observation so far). But this clearly will not work for reason-explanations: both because we are not dealing with generalizations, but with specific reasons on a particular occasion, and because we cannot *observe* someone's reasons in the same straightforward way as we can observe preceding movements. We are back with the problem of 'other minds'. If, when you ask me 'Why do you say you trust Mr Smith?', I reply, 'It's because he has such a trustworthy manner', then you cannot tell, *just by looking*, that that is my real reason for saying it. In many cases, moreover, we give reason-explanations without relying on what the agent says. So how do we decide on a reason-explanation of someone's actions?

Some of the philosophers referred to above, such as Dilthey and Weber, and the British philosopher R. G. Collingwood, connected understanding with what is sometimes called 'empathy'. Their idea was that, in order to discover what someone's reason for acting was, we should, as it were, put ourselves in the agent's shoes and think his or her thoughts about the matter. There is obviously something in this: we can often work out why someone did something by asking ourselves what might have influenced us to act in that way if we had been in that person's situation. The difficulty, however, is over how literally we should take the idea of 'thinking another person's thoughts for ourselves'. The idea of the subjectivity of thought means that we *cannot* literally think another person's thoughts. And, as we saw in the last chapter, if we accept Cartesian dualism, we cannot 'get inside' another person's mind to think his or her thoughts. So how do we do this trick?

We might follow up the lead suggested by the discussion in the previous chapter about our knowledge of other minds. To see what reasons someone might have had for doing something – say, going for a walk – we need to see what kinds of reasons might make it intelligible for someone in that person's situation to do this. And intelligible reasons are those that are generally accepted as being such – some of the intelligible reasons for going for a walk have been listed above (getting exercise, relaxing, enjoying the countryside and so on). We all know that these are generally accepted in our culture as reasons for performing that particular kind of activity which we call 'going for a walk'. What we need to know is which of these intelligible reasons was *this person's* reason *in that situation*. For that, we need to know, not just what the 'objective' features of the situation were, but *how that person saw* that situation. To know the latter, we need to know something more about that person.

Suppose we know, for instance, that this person just loves to take exercise in the fresh air, and that she has been cooped up indoors doing sedentary work all day: that makes it likely that a primary reason she would have for going for a walk at that point would be to get some fresh air and exercise. Using our imagination and our wider knowledge of her to try to work out how she would see her present situation is what we express metaphorically by 'putting ourselves in her place'. (As we saw in Chapter 5, we may never be certain that we have understood her reasons correctly.)

Some philosophers who do not much like the distinction between causal and reason-explanation, such as Karl Popper, argue that putting ourselves in her place is just a way of discovering general hypotheses about what causes her to act which we can then apply to give a straightforward causal explanation. But that doesn't seem to be right. We do not formulate some generalization such as 'People of her type who have been indoors and inactive for a certain length of time tend to go for walks', thus hypothesizing that the time spent indoors and inactive is the cause of her going for a walk. Even if she is of that 'type', she might react to the time spent indoors differently: going jogging, for example. If this is her reason for going for a walk, it is because *she herself sees* it as such: she makes a connection on this occasion (maybe not on others) between being cooped up indoors and going for a walk to 'blow the cobwebs off'. Understanding is particular to the individual and the case, not based on generalizations about types. And that is why understanding of reasons is appropriate to actions in which 'mind' is involved.

The standards of intelligibility of reasons are determined by the culture to which the person acting and the person trying to understand the action belong: as said earlier, intelligible reasons for acting are those which are generally accepted as such. Some, though, seem to be universal to all members of the human species, because dependent on human biology. We all get hungry, for example, so we can all understand, independently of culture, that someone might pluck an apple from a tree because he was hungry. We all need sleep, so we can all see, independently of culture, that someone might stop working because she was tired. But all our standards of intelligibility are tied to culture, whether it is human culture in general or a particular local culture to which we happen to belong. A culture could be defined, from one point of view, as a system of standards of what counts as intelligible reasons for acting. For this reason, a philosopher like Dilthey calls a culture 'Objective Mind', mind as realized in collective institutions and practices, and distinguishes the 'human' sciences, such as history, sociology or economics, which seek to understand human beings as members of a culture, from a 'natural' science, such as biology, which seeks to give causal explanations of the physical movements of living things, and in which human beings are regarded as just another species of animal.

III

So is this Cartesian dualism in another form? It certainly doesn't seem to require us to think of 'minds' as separate, inner worlds which we have to penetrate to explain human behaviour. Rather, we understand what people do, in those cases in which their minds are involved, by using our imagination and by reference to the shared standards of intelligibility which we have by participating in a culture. A classical materialist, however, might want to argue that this distinction between reasons and causes is still unacceptably dualist, even if it is not Cartesian. For it seems to be guilty of denying the possibility of integrating our explanation of human behaviour with the rest of our scientific understanding of the world. If the study of human psychology is distinct from the study of human biology, to the extent that the laws which explain human movement play no part in the explanation of human intentional action, then that does seem to imply that our mental lives are separate from our lives as physical beings. Some philosophers have attempted to bridge this gap by assimilating reason-explanation to a special variety of causal explanation: for them, 'reasons' are just a rather peculiar kind of 'cause'. This sounds plausible in some ways: after all, to use our earlier example, someone's going for a walk could be said to be 'brought about' by her desire for exercise.

But in other ways, the parallel does not seem to hold. Reason-explanations do not seem, as we have seen, to be based on general laws, as causal explanations are. And even if such laws do exist and could be found if we thought hard enough (which seems doubtful), we do not need them in order to explain this person's going for a walk on this occasion. Once we have been told her reason for doing so, as long as it is an intelligible one, we have a perfectly satisfactory understanding of why she went for a walk, regardless of what might be true about her psychological type. More importantly, even if general laws do come into play somewhere in the background, it is not clear that they make our reason-explanation into a form of causal explanation. Reason-explanations are connected with intentionality. She can have a desire to get exercise by going for a walk only if she has the concept of getting exercise in this way – only if she sees what she is doing under that description. Seeing what she is doing as 'a way of taking exercise' cannot be explained by the brain-processes, or any other internal processes, which go on before it, since to have a concept is to have learned to use a certain expression ('getting exercise by going for a walk') in social interactions with other human beings. These social interactions take the form of learning to recognize when it is correct to describe what someone is doing in this way and when it is incorrect: in other words, recognizing certain social norms. These norms are not actually existing objects. They exist only in so far as they are recognized by human beings as providing possible reasons for action, so they can't *cause* their own recognition. So having this as a reason for acting is not being caused to act, either by internal processes or by social conditioning, but is acting in a way which is intelligible because it conforms to social norms.

Another way of closing the gap would be to deny that human action needs a special kind of explanation. In many ways, this is another way of seeing the eliminativist programme of doing away with 'folk psychology' in favour of a 'completed neuroscience'. To examine this proposal in this new light, we should go back to some of the criticisms of folk psychology made by Churchland. He gives a number of examples of the failures of folk psychology as a scientific theory of human behaviour, as we saw in Chapter 2. Let us recall some of the cases he picks out particularly: the nature and dynamics of mental illness; creative imagination; and the differences in intelligence between different individuals. These three cases are similar in two interesting ways. First, they all clearly belong in the domain of psychology – they concern people as what we have called 'psychological beings', so there is an obvious need to see how they fit with what has just been said about reason-explanation. Secondly, they are difficult to fit in, if only because they seem to require some reference to the functioning of the brain in their explanation.

That second point needs some elaboration. We can take the three examples in turn. First, mental illness. Mental illness is by definition an *abnormality* of thought, feeling or behaviour. 'Normal' thought, feeling and behaviour is behaviour which most people find it possible to understand. If someone, for instance, feels 'down' because they have just failed an important examination, then that is normal. If we ask them why they feel down, and they give this reason for being in that mood, then we can fairly easily understand their feelings (even if we ourselves have never felt 'down' in that situation). This is, in other words, an intelligible reason-explanation. But if they say they feel depressed because they are so worthless, then we find that, to say the least, harder to understand – especially if there seems no obvious reason for them to have that low opinion of themselves. Here we may be faced with a case of *clinical* depression, a mental disorder rather than a normal mood. The very fact that they give such an unintelligible answer to our question 'Why?' seems to require explanation. The fact that it is unintelligible means that we cannot readily give reasons for it, so it seems natural to conclude that the explanation must be *causal*. One possible causal explanation for this strange way of thinking might be that it resulted from some disease of or injury to the person's brain: and this may be the kind of thing which Churchland means by saying that the nature and dynamics of mental illness cannot be adequately explained by folk-psychology, but require to be explained by neuroscience.

The second example concerns creative imagination. We could take as an illustration of the idea of creative imagination the work of a novelist like Tolkien, in writing a work of fantasy, like his *The Lord of the Rings.* Tolkien here created an entirely imaginary world, populated by beings very different from any creatures we actually find in the real world. He may well, of course, have derived some of the materials of his fantasy world from other sources such as old myths and fairy stories, but the way he put these materials together was entirely new and entirely his own. If we ask 'Why did Tolkien create this particular world, rather than any other?', could folk-psychology give us an answer in the form of a reason-explanation? The answer seems to be 'No': the whole point of saying that his work was 'creative' is that it does not conform to any recognized norms. We less creative people could not say that this is what we should have done in the same situation: indeed, we find it impossible to understand how Tolkien's mind must have worked, and can only marvel at his imagination. If folk-psychology cannot explain creativity, Churchland seems to be saying, then maybe a completed neuroscience could – by for example exhibiting the peculiar brain structures which creative people may have which enable them to put together material in new and unheard of ways.

Finally, there are the differences in intelligence between different individuals. However difficult it may be to define or therefore to measure intelligence, there seems little doubt that some people are more intelligent than others, or at least have more intelligence of a particular kind than others. They have more of a capacity for reasoning things through, or for developing new and original ideas, or for finding solutions to problems and so on. It seems equally clear that we cannot give a reason-explanation of these differences: and that is so clear simply because reason-explanations are supposed to be given for having particular thoughts, feelings and actions, whereas intelligence is a matter of *how* someone thinks or acts. We could perhaps answer the question 'Why did he think this?' by giving his reasons for thinking it. But that would not explain why his thinking was as *intelligent* as it was: that is a different question, requiring a different kind of explanation. Neuroscience on the other hand *might* be able to answer the second question: it might be that we could give a causal explanation of intelligence in terms of the presence of certain features or structures in the brains of more intelligent people which are not found, or are not so developed, in less intelligent people.

IV

So there is at least some plausibility in Churchland's claims about these three examples. Does it follow that he is right in his general thesis that folk-psychology is a primitive type of explanatory theory which needs to be replaced, and will eventually be replaced, by a completed neuroscience? The answer which I want to give to this question is in two parts. First, if we take the field of human psychology to which reason-explanation is intended to apply, he has given us no reason for abandoning it in favour of causal explanations based on neuroscience. The proper field of reason-explanation is normal human actions, where by 'normal' I mean 'conforming to some generally accepted norm of intelligibility'. The examples which Churchland gives, and which we have discussed above, do not come within this proper field, and so have no bearing on the validity or usefulness of what he calls 'folk-psychology'. As was said above in the discussion of mental illness, for instance, we can readily understand the normal feelings which we call depression, because they are responses to situations which we could conceivably experience ourselves. What seems to baffle us is the depressive response which we cannot make sense of in these terms. The cases of creative imagination and differences in intelligence seem to fall outside the scope of reason-explanation in a different way – that they concern unusual *capacities* rather than human *actions*. The fact that reason-explanation does not apply to them, therefore, says nothing about its usefulness in its own proper field.

If we stick to the proper field of reason-explanation, furthermore, we can make a more positive point. Within that field, 'folk-psychology' is actually *superior* to neuroscience – it enables us to explain things which neuroscience cannot. By abandoning terms like 'reason', 'desire', 'wish', 'intention' and so on, and replacing them by terms like 'neuron-firings', the completed neuroscience which Churchland envisages would make it impossible to distinguish between different actions performed with the same physical movements. Two men kick a football with their right leg, applying the same degree of force. Their leg movements in both cases can no doubt be causally explained as the outcome of messages from the appropriate part of the brain reaching their foot by means of their nervous system. But one of them is a professional footballer who kicks the ball in the direction of the goal in the course of a match, while the other is a father kicking the ball idly while playing with his children in the park. Neuroscience cannot distinguish these two cases, and can explain only in the sense of saying how it came about in each case that the man's foot moved in the way it did. But the movements in each case were part of the performance of a different action. We can ask of the actions, 'Why did he do it?': the answer in one case would be 'In an attempt to kick a goal and so put his team in the lead', and in the other 'As part of a casual kick-around with his children'. The reason-explanation allows us to understand this difference, in a way that the causal explanation does not.

So even if what Churchland says about his three examples is correct, it does not follow that folk-psychology is past its sell-by date and needs to be substituted by a more neuroscientifically based study of human behaviour. This leads us on to the second part of my answer to the question, which involves asking another question. How much force, in fact, is there in Churchland's claims about the superiority of neuroscience, even in the examples which we have discussed? We need to take the case of mental illness separately from the other two, because it raises somewhat different issues. Abnormal thoughts, feelings, moods and behaviour clearly can't be understood in terms of normal standards (this is almost true by definition). When the person with clinical depression says that she feels utterly worthless and unfit to go on living, we feel both distressed and baffled. It would take a lot to make us think that *anyone's* life was utterly worthless, and nothing about her that we know would justify that feeling or make it 'rational'. So why does she feel that way? One example of an explanation which would fit in with Churchland's claims would be that depression is caused by decreased concentration of a neuro-transmitter (roughly, a brain chemical) called serotonin – a decreased concentration which itself may ultimately have genetic origins. (Explanations along these lines are favoured by many contemporary psychiatrists.) This, it is suggested, would make depression into an essentially biological condition, similar to a bodily illness. But this is not the only explanation that has been offered. Many favour 'cognitive' theories of depression, according to which it is a form of 'learned helplessness': the person has been faced, according to these theories, by some misfortune with which they could not deal in any positive or constructive way, and has therefore simply given up trying (adopted a strategy of being helpless). 'Psychodynamic' theories, on the other hand, see depression as a kind of mourning for the loss of certain attachment figures, that is, people to whom one was attached in early childhood. Both cognitive and psychodynamic theories are attempts to *understand* the reasons for depression, the meaning which it has for the depressed person.

It might be said, and rightly, that which of these theories is correct is an empirical matter, not one to be settled by philosophical argument. But the point here is not to say which is correct, but only to show that it is perfectly possible to explain the 'nature and dynamics' of at least one major mental illness in terms of the agent's reasons. These reasons may be difficult to understand, but it is not impossible to do so with some effort of the imagination; and the explanations can be tested by their success as a basis for therapy (in fact cognitively based therapies are widely acknowledged to play a useful part in the treatment of depression). And there is a further point which might be made. Mental disorders differ in one significant way from bodily illnesses: they crucially affect thoughts, feelings, moods and actions, rather than bodily mechanisms (or, if they do affect bodily mechanisms, it is *via* their effect on thoughts, feelings, moods and behaviour). Thoughts, feelings, moods and actions require reasons, even if the reasons which the agent gives deviate from the normal. For example, to say that the depressive person's mood is irrational is not to say that the person has *no* reasons for feeling that way, but that the reasons the person offers fail to meet normal standards of reasonableness: putting it in a paradoxical form, we need to understand it in the sense of seeing that it is difficult to understand.

If what is disordered about depression could be defined in simple biological terms, then depression would consist in nothing more than bodily processes which were dysfunctional in sustaining life and ordinary levels of activity, and then it could perhaps be causally explained. That is the assumption behind the theory that a decreased concentration of serotonin in the brain offers a complete explanation of depression. That decreased concentration of serotonin is regularly found conjoined with depressive moods is an empirical hypothesis which philosophy can neither confirm nor deny. If it is confirmed (and there seems to be good empirical evidence for it), and if saying that A and B are constantly conjoined is, as Hume says, equivalent to saying that A causes B, then neuroscience can legitimately say that decreased serotonin concentrations cause depression (or perhaps vice versa). No purely philosophical argument could undermine that. What philosophy can do, however, is to suggest that depression as a human condition, a mental disorder, seems to require understanding rather than, or as well as, causal explanation. In that way, again, folk-psychology would not have been superseded by neuroscience.

If we turn now to the other two examples, of creative imagination and differences in intelligence, the argument is different. Even the strongest defender of folk-psychology could accept that it is impossible to 'understand' these psychological phenomena. But this is not a failure of folk-psychology, since, as said already, these are not cases of human actions which could be explained in terms of their agents' reasons, but of the existence of human capacities, which are natural facts like any other. The only possible explanation for them must be causal, and almost certainly in terms of brain structures and functioning, that is, of neuroscience. Churchland has made his case that folk-psychology cannot deal with these aspects of psychology, but not that that means it is a failed theory, due for replacement by neuroscience.

If we accept these arguments, then the only possible justification for eliminating folk-psychology is a general belief in the ideal of a unified science. But in what sense does science need to be unified? We saw in Chapter 2 how a major portion of the inspiration for classical materialism was a dislike of 'nomological danglers': explanations of certain special types of phenomena which could not be logically related to the explanations of others. An example which is often cited is the old 'vitalist' idea that the workings of living organisms could not be fully explained in terms of the laws of physics and chemistry which we use to explain the behaviour of inorganic matter. The vitalists believed that there were special forces at work in living beings, a special 'life-force' which was purposive in nature, and so gave a different type of explanation of living phenomena: the workings of the heart in the human body, for example, had to be explained in terms of its *function* in sustaining the life of the body, and vitalists took that to mean in terms of the *purpose* which it fulfilled. Opponents of vitalism objected to it on the grounds of a principle that we have already mentioned, that of 'Occam's Razor' – the principle that entities must not be multiplied beyond necessity.

Occam's Razor is attractive because it recommends that we make our theories as neat and elegant as we can. The problem with vitalism was that it made our world too messy, by crowding it out with all sorts of extra entities ('life-forces' and the like), which it would be better to avoid. If we can explain the workings of the heart, for example, perfectly well in terms of more ordinary, observable things, of the kind that physics and chemistry study, then that makes things much less messy. Cartesian dualism is similarly inelegant: it introduces extra entities called 'minds' or 'souls', in order to explain certain things about human behaviour, and these things can't be observed in the usual way or experimentally studied. Wouldn't it be better, neater, therefore, if we could explain everything about human behaviour without invoking anything except things we *can* observe and study experimentally, and which behave in accordance with the ordinary laws of physics and chemistry – neurons, for example? If the demand for the unity of science meant simply that we should use Occam's Razor, then it is easy to see its appeal.

But does folk-psychology require the existence of extra, unobservable entities? Not necessarily. To say that human actions need to be understood in terms of their reasons, while bodily movements can be causally explained, does not entail that there are two distinct types of thing, 'actions' and 'bodily movements', the first of which, unlike the second, is unobservable. When we see someone acting in a certain way, we also see them moving in particular ways. If I see a friend going for a walk (an action), I also see her body moving – her legs moving backwards and forwards, and so on. Since we are embodied beings, as Merleau-Ponty reminds us, we cannot perform actions without bodily movements of any kind. We cannot even think or feel without at least the occurrence of some internal bodily movements, especially in the brain. If damage of some kind affects the workings of our brain, or our capacities for bodily movement, then we cannot perform relevant actions at all (or in milder cases, can perform them only in a form which falls short of what may be regarded as satisfactory). If we are paralysed from the neck down, we cannot go for a walk; if we have arthritic knees, we can walk only unsteadily and with discomfort. If the parts of our brain involved in short-term memory are seriously damaged, we lose the ability to remember what happened a few minutes ago. If memory centres are less severely damaged, we have only impaired memories. So distinguishing actions from movements is not identifying two different types of entities, one of them unobservable.

What does the distinction involve then? If there is a distinction at all, it must at least involve different ways of thinking and talking about what we observe. An action may be possible only if some bodily movements or other can take place, but it cannot be equated with any single specific set of bodily movements. We can perform the same action with different bodily movements, and the same bodily movements can be involved in different actions. The action of greeting a friend, for instance, can be performed by waving one's hand, nodding one's head, smiling, shouting 'Hello!', embracing them and in many other ways. And waving one's hand may not only be greeting someone, but also, say, brushing a wasp away from one's head. To say what someone is doing may be, in one context, to describe the action they are performing, but in another to describe the bodily movement they are performing ('He's greeting his friend', 'He's moving his arms about over his head'). Both descriptions may be true: but which is appropriate will be determined by the context, including our background knowledge of the circumstances. Thus, we might prefer to describe what he is doing as 'Moving his arms above his head' if we were either physiologists of some kind interested in studying human arm-movements, or uncertain about *why* he was waving his arms, so that we preferred this more neutral description. Or, even if we knew why, we might describe what he is doing as 'Just moving his arms' if, for instance, we didn't like the man and didn't want to acknowledge that he was greeting us.

Which description we choose is important, among other reasons, because it determines what kind of explanation it is appropriate to give. If we say that what he is doing is 'Moving his arms', we could give a causal explanation, in terms of what brought it about that his arms moved as they did (what went on in his brain, nervous system, muscles, etc., which led, in accordance with ordinary laws of physiology, to these movements of his limbs through space). If we describe him as performing an action, on the other hand – '*Waving* his arms', in this case – then it would be silly to answer the question 'Why is he waving them?' in terms of physiological movements. The only appropriate answer would be in terms of his reasons for acting in that way (something like 'He's greeting Sam, his good friend'). In order to say that the causal explanation of his movements is plausible, we need to know something about the laws of physiology; in order to say that the reason-explanation is plausible, we need to know about the conventional ways of greeting someone in this society, and that waving to them is one possible way (we also need to know, for instance, that Sam *is* indeed a good friend of the man and other similar facts about the individual situation). What has been said about actions applies equally, with appropriate changes, to thoughts, feelings, moods, and other intentional activities, processes and states.

But aren't reasons extra, unobservable entities? We can observe, in principle at least, the physiological causes of his movements, and the constant conjunction between events of these two types: but can we observe his reasons – aren't they extra entities lurking somewhere undetectable behind the scenes? It has already been argued in this book that they are not. We can discover what his reasons are, at least in many cases, by observing the *manner* of his actions and their *context*. If we know that he is a friend of Sam's, and if, after waving, he goes across to her and embraces her, and if there is no other plausible reason for waving his arms in the context, then it becomes almost certain that that is why he was waving – as certain as any physiological explanation of his arm movements. Of course, as was also said before, in more complex and subtle cases, there may be much more room for doubt. If we want to know the reason for the Mona Lisa's smile, there are many theories on offer, and none of them can be conclusively accepted as correct: the smile remains inscrutable. But it is so, not because her reason for smiling like that is an extra hidden and in principle unobservable entity, but simply because we know very little, almost nothing, about her and her life, and about the context in which she smiled as she does in the painting.

The difference in the forms of explanation favoured by folk-psychology and neuroscience thus does not depend on the fact that folk-psychology adds unnecessary entities to the world, while neuro-science sticks with those which we all recognize as the minimum necessary for us to make sense of the world. Rather, it depends on the recognition that there are different ways of making sense of the world which are appropriate in different contexts. If the belief in the unity of science means a belief that there is only one 'scientific' way to make sense of the world, and that difference of context is irrelevant, then that belief seems much less plausible. Science just means 'rational knowledge of things', and it is surely rational to acknowledge that there are different ways in which we can make sense of things, depending on the context and our interests. To repeat a point made earlier, a physiological account of the causes of waving movements of the arm will not explain why one arm movement is a greeting and the other (physiologically exactly similar) is an attempt to get rid of a wasp from the person's head. Where physiology, or neuroscience, may be relevant to the explanation of action, in a roundabout way, is to the *absence* of a capacity to act. Thus, to explain why someone sees the past through rose-tinted spectacles, we need to understand her reasons for doing so: but to see how it comes about that someone cannot remember the past at all, we shall almost certainly need to look at damage to their brain through disease or injury.

Now that we are coming to the end of this book, we can return to the question that we started with. What does it mean to have a mind? If the arguments put forward in this and preceding chapters are accepted, it means, as Merleau-Ponty would put it, to be an embodied subject: a human being, or similar creature, who is a biological organism, but who also responds to his or her environment subjectively and intentionally. To be embodied, but not a subject, would be to relate to the world passively and in accordance with universal laws: as a potato, for example, is affected by the world, but does not act on it. How the potato relates to the rain which falls on it, for instance, is determined, not by the way the potato *sees* the rain (it doesn't see it at all), but by the universal laws governing the way in which damp affects matter of this kind. For the same reason, there is nothing *individual* about the potato's response – nothing which makes it *its own* response and not that of some other (that's why the potato is an 'it' and not a 'he' or a 'she'). Human beings, however, and perhaps some other animals, do respond, at least to some extent, individually to their worlds, and in ways governed by how they *see* their world – what 'meaning' they find in it.

To say that human beings have minds, on this view, is not to say that they have an extra bit in their composition, a non-physical soul. It is quite compatible with accepting what science seems to tell us, that human beings are animals of a certain species, and that as such they operate in many respects like any other living being. This means that many of their operations can be fully explained by the laws of physics and chemistry, and their derivatives in biology. But it does not follow from that that human beings are machines, or that machines could have minds in the way human beings do. The most characteristically human parts of human behaviour, it has been argued, are those which require to be understood in terms of their meaning for the person in question, rather than causally explained by physico-chemical laws. These are the parts which are most relevant for our lives together as human beings, rather than for a purely objective scientific study of human beings as just one other type of object in the world. However valid and indeed important that scientific study may be, it is the 'subjective' and the 'intentional' about human behaviour, in other words, the human mind, which we value when we value humanity. To say that human beings have minds is precisely to deny that they are mere machines.

That is what we should conclude if we accept the arguments put forward in this book, including the arguments against alternative views. But it has to be admitted that, as always in philosophy, those arguments against alternative views can never amount to conclusive disproof. Philosophy is not about proof or disproof, or about final truth: but it is about accepting views only to the extent that one finds the balance of the arguments coming down on their side.

REFERENCES

Aristotle (1986), *De Anima*, trans. Hugh Lawson-Tancred. Harmondsworth: Penguin Classics.

Churchland, Paul (2004), 'Eliminative materialism and the propositional attitudes', in John Heil (ed.), *Philosophy of Mind: A guide and anthology*, Oxford: Oxford University Press, pp. 382–400.

Dennett, Daniel C. (1991), *Consciousness Explained*, London: Allen Lane, The Penguin Press.

Descartes (1984), *The Philosophical Writings of Descartes*, trans. John Cottingham, Robert Stoothoff and Dugald Murdoch, Cambridge: Cambridge University Press, Vol. II.

Descartes (1985), *The Philosophical Writings of Descartes* [as above], Vol. I.

Fodor, Jerry (2004), 'The mind–body problem', in John Heil (ed.), *Philosophy of Mind: A guide and anthology*, Oxford: Oxford University Press, pp. 168–82.

Kripke, Saul (1980), *Naming and Necessity*, Oxford: Basil Blackwell.

La Mettrie (1996), *Machine Man and Other Writings*, trans. and ed. Ann Thomson, Cambridge: Cambridge University Press.

Merleau-Ponty, Maurice (1965), *The Structure of Behaviour*, trans. Alden L. Fisher, London: Methuen.

Moran, Dermot and Mooney, Timothy (eds) (2002), *The Phenomenology Reader*, London and New York: Routledge.

Place, U. T. (2002), 'Is consciousness a brain-process?', in David J. Chalmers (ed.), *Philosophy of Mind: Classical and Contemporary Readings*, New York and Oxford: Oxford University Press, pp. 55–60.

Ryle, Gilbert (1990), *The Concept of Mind*, London: Penguin Books.

Searle, John (1997), *The Mystery of Consciousness*, London: Granta Books.

Searle, John (1999), *Mind, Language and Society: Philosophy in the Real World*, London: Weidenfeld & Nicolson.

Smart, J. J. C. (2004), 'Sensations and brain-processes', reprinted in J. Heil (ed.), *Philosophy of Mind: A guide and anthology*, Oxford: Oxford University Press pp. 116–127.

Strawson, P. F. (1959), *Individuals*, London: Methuen.

Wittgenstein, Ludwig (1953), *Philosophical Investigations*, trans. G. E. M. Anscombe, Oxford: Basil Blackwell.

INDEX